Embroidery

May Gibbs
Embroidery

Designs by Alison Snepp

BayBooks

An imprint of HarperCollins*Publishers*

Flowers by Lisa Milasas

Contents

Flowers by Lisa Milasas

Introduction

May Gibbs was born Cecilia May Gibbs in Surrey, England, in 1877. In 1881 she emigrated to Australia with her parents and brothers. As a child she was actively encouraged by her parents to draw. Her first book, *Snugglepot and Cuddlepie*, was published in 1918 and has never been out of print. May went on to create more wonderful stories and characters which have entertained children and adults alike ever since.

Still Australia's most well-loved children's author and illustrator, her friendly bush creatures and adorable flower babies have become popular icons of Australian culture and remain a symbol of the beauty and fragility of the Australian bush.

Copyright of all May Gibbs' work rests with the Spastic Centre of New South Wales and the New South Wales Society for Children and Young Adults with Physical Disabilities and they are recipients of all royalties from the sale of this book. These beautiful projects inspired by May Gibbs' illustrations and stories are intended for personal use and not for any commercial purpose. They have been designed with the approval and co-operation of the copyright holders and their agents, Curtis Brown (Australia) Pty Ltd.

General instructions

Needles

Tapestry needles should be used for all the counted-thread projects in this book. Tapestry needles are fairly thick and have a blunt end, which means that they will not catch the fabric as they pass through the holes. Crewel needles are used for the Shadow Work projects in the book. These needles are sharp and have an elongated eye.

Hoops and frames

Counted-thread embroidery does not have to be done on an embroidery hoop or frame, but some embroiderers prefer to use one. It is often easier to find the holes while stitching if the evenweave fabric is laced firmly onto a frame or held tightly in a hoop. The Shadow Work projects in the book must be done on an embroidery hoop. The fine fabric should be held taut at all times while the embroidery is being worked, to stop the stitches being pulled too tightly and distorting the delicate fabric. Remove the fabric from the hoop when it is not being worked.

The canvas work cushion in this book must be worked on a roller frame, to hold the canvas straight and taut. The method for mounting the canvas on the frame is given in the project instructions.

Chart markers

A chart marker is a metal sheet with magnetic strips that are used to hold the chart in position and indicate the row being worked. Move the magnetic strips across the chart as the embroidery progresses. A chart marker is an invaluable tool, particularly when the embroidery is picked up and put down frequently, and when a large chart is being worked.

Magnifiers

A magnifier may help you to work the finer linens and Aida fabrics. There are two types of magnifiers available. One is simply a magnifying glass attached to a cord; the cord is placed around your neck and supports the magnifier, which sits on your chest. These magnifiers are lightweight and portable.

You can also obtain magnifiers which are incorporated into lights. The magnifying lens sits in the centre of a circular fluorescent tube, or alongside a fluorescent or incandescent globe. These magnifiers are usually attached to an extendable arm which can be clamped onto a table or fitted to a stand on castors.

A specialist needlework shop or a lighting store can advise you on which magnifier will suit you.

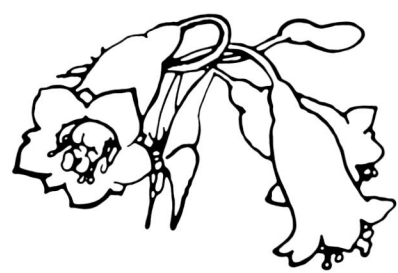

Stitch instructions

The counted-thread embroidery designs in this book are shown in chart form. One square on the chart represents one stitch on the fabric or canvas. Each symbol shown within each square on the chart represents a colour. Refer to the chart's key to see which colour is represented by which symbol. The Shadow Work designs in the book are shown as line drawings. The colours to be used are shown in the key. The line drawings should be lightly traced onto the right side of the fabric using a sharp HB pencil.

Cross Stitch

It is important when working Cross Stitch that each stitch is worked in the same manner, so that the second parts of all stitches are always in the same direction. Use a tapestry needle in the size specified for all Cross Stitch projects in this book.

Bring the needle up through the fabric at the lower left-hand side of the stitch. Count over two threads of linen (or one bundle of Aida fabric) to the right and two threads (one bundle) up, and put the needle into the fabric at this point. In the same movement, count two threads (one bundle) directly down and bring the needle out through the fabric. This is a half Cross Stitch (see diagram, Cross Stitch 1).

Cross Stitch 1

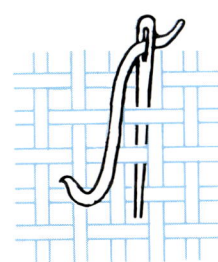

 Count to the right over two threads (one bundle) from where the top of the last stitch went into the fabric and put the needle in here, bringing it out two threads (one bundle) below (see diagram, Cross Stitch 2).

Cross Stitch 2

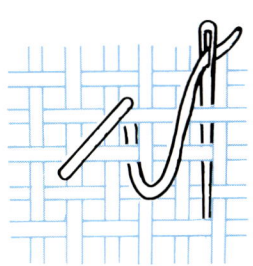

Work along a row in this manner until as many half stitches have been worked as are indicated in the colour area in that row on the chart.

Without turning the embroidery, work back across the row, crossing each stitch into the same holes as the first half of the Cross Stitches (see diagrams, Cross Stitch 3 and 4.)

Cross Stitch 3

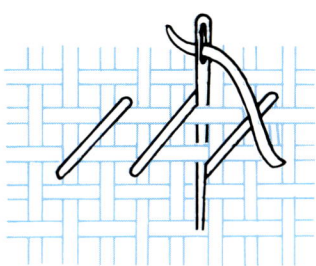

Cross Stitch 4

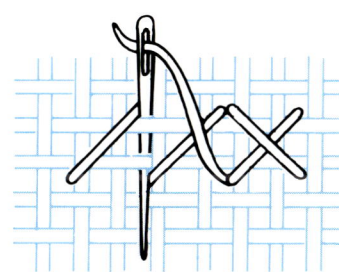

ENDING OFF: To end off Cross Stitch, finish the stitch being worked, take the needle through to the back of the work, and then run the needle underneath five or six vertical stitches on the back of the work (see diagram, Cross Stitch 5). If the embroidered project is to be washed frequently, it is a good idea to run the needle back under four verticals to lock the threads more securely.

Cross Stitch 5: ending off

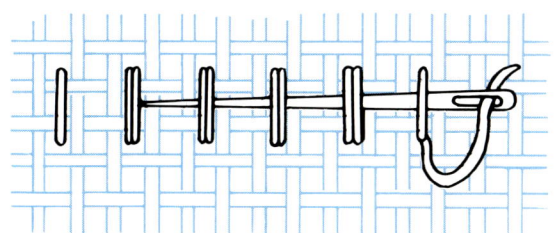

Double Running Stitch (Holbein Stitch)

Double Running Stitch is most useful for outlining areas of Cross Stitch, and for working straight lines, as it looks the same on the back as on the front. Use a tapestry needle for all Double Running Stitch.

This stitch is simply a running stitch worked over and under the number of threads or bundles shown on the chart (see diagram, Double Running Stitch 1).

Double Running Stitch 1

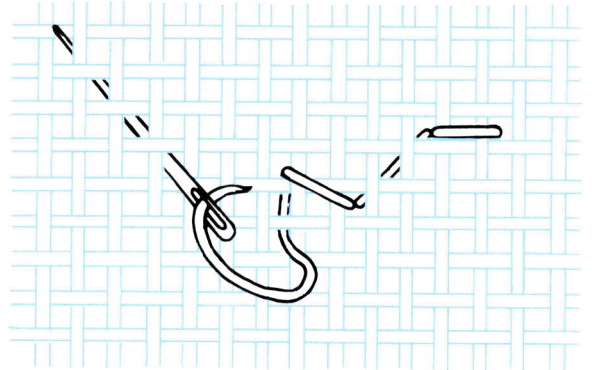

Turn the work around, and work the running stitch back to fill in the gaps left on the first pass of running stitch (see diagram, Double Running Stitch 2).

Double Running Stitch 2

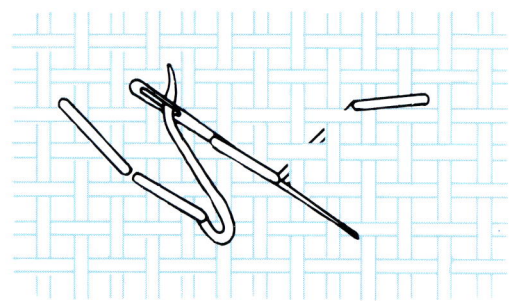

If Double Running Stitch is to be worked as an outline, as in Assisi work, always work the Cross Stitch first, then the Double Running Stitch, otherwise the Cross Stitch will cover the outline.

ENDING OFF: Finish a stitch, take the needle through to the back of the work, and whip over and over through five or six stitches.

Shadow Work

Shadow embroidery is easy to work from the right side of the fabric, using Back Stitch which is worked alternately from one side to the other in the stitch area. A fine crewel needle (size 9 or 10) and one strand of stranded embroidery thread should be used for Shadow embroidery.

Bring the needle up through the fabric, a little distance to the left of the end of one line. Put the needle in at the end of the line (that is, a little to the right of where the thread comes out of the fabric) and bring the needle out of the fabric on the other line, a little to the left of the end of the other line (see diagram, Shadow Work 1).

Shadow Work 1

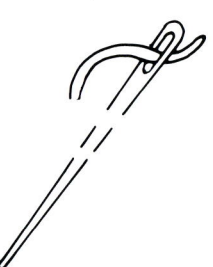

Put the needle down into the fabric again at the end of the same line (see diagram, Shadow Work 2).

Shadow Work 2

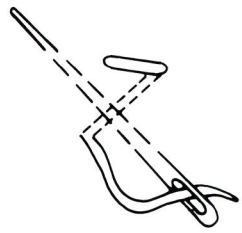

Bring the needle up again on the first line, a little to the left of the last stitch on the first line, and put the needle down into the fabric again in the same hole where the first Back Stitch ended (see diagram, Shadow Work 3).

Shadow Work 3

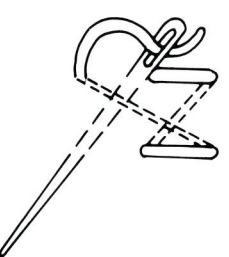

Continue in this manner, working Back Stitches alternately on one line and then the other. It is the thread taken from one side to the other which gives the shadow effect.

When working a curved area of Shadow embroidery, the Back Stitches will have to be shorter on the shorter line and longer on the longer line so that the further end of the curved shape is reached at the same time by both sides.

ENDING OFF: Complete a stitch, take the needle through to the back of the work and carefully run the needle through the back of the stitches, splitting the embroidery thread behind the Back Stitches.

Hem Stitch

Hem Stitch is a stitch which is pulled tightly to bring together in bundles the threads around which each stitch is worked. For the Hem Stitching in this book, use a tapestry needle and ecru machine thread.

Hold the hem towards you so that the bulk of the fabric is away from you. You will be working this stitch from the left corner, towards the right. Starting at the bottom left-hand corner, bring the needle up through the hem on the fabric an even number of threads from the corner of the hem (see diagram, Hem Stitch1). Leave a starting length of about 9 or 10 cm on the back of the work. This should be ended-off after the length of thread is complete, following the ending-off instructions.

Count to the right over two threads in the single layer of fabric, then two threads up, and put the needle in here, bringing it out two threads to the left of where the needle went in (see diagram, Hem Stitch 1). This should be level with where the thread is coming out in the hem.

Hem Stitch 1

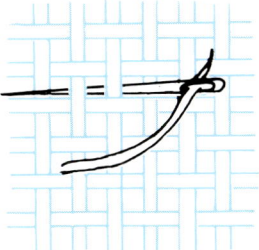

Put the needle into the hem, two threads to the right of where the thread comes out (this is the same hole where the last stitch went into the hem), and bring it out two threads directly below (see diagram, Hem Stitch 2). Pull thread tightly.

Hem Stitch 2

Put the needle into the single layer of fabric again, two threads to the right of the last stitch, bringing it out two threads to the left (see diagram, Hem Stitch 3). Pull the thread tightly. Repeat until the length to be Hem Stitched is complete.

Hem Stitch 3

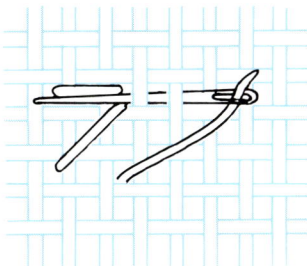

The even, firm tension on the thread must be maintained while Hem Stitching, in order to pull the threads evenly together into bundles.

ENDING OFF: Work a row of running stitches back between the two threads around which the Hem Stitching has been worked. The row of running stitches should be over and under about 15 individual threads in the fabric. Starting threads should be finished off in the same manner.

Back Stitch

Back Stitch is used for outline detail in some of the designs in the book. Back Stitch can be worked in several directions (see diagram, Back Stitch). The straight outline drawn on the chart will show the direction required. Use two threads for all the Back Stitch in this book. Two threads on the illustration are the same as one bundle of Aida fabric.

Back Stitch

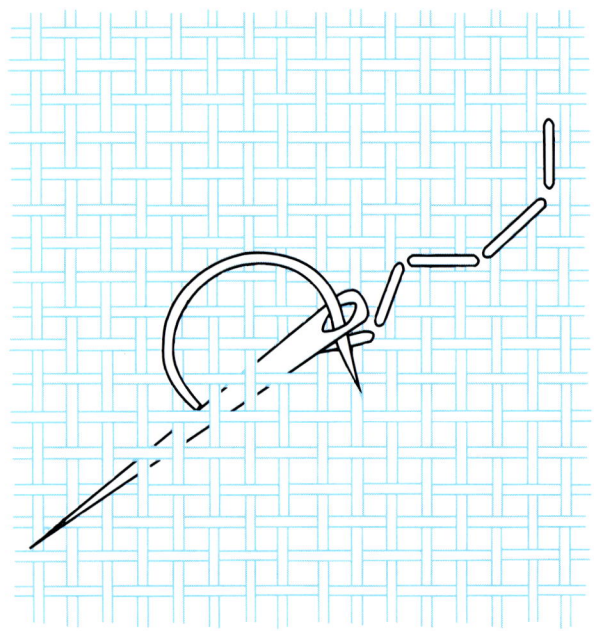

ENDING OFF: Finish a stitch, take the needle through to the back of the work, and whip over and over through five or six stitches.

Continental Stitch

Each Continental Stitch covers one intersection of canvas and lies in an oblique direction sloping from lower left to top right (see diagram, Continental Stitch). When working a row from right to left, bring the needle up through the canvas at 1, count over and up one thread and push the needle back down through the canvas at 2. Bring the needle up through the canvas at 3, down at 4 and so on.

Continental Stitch

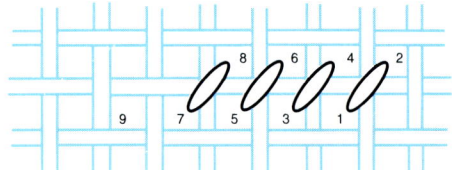

When working from left to right, turn the stitch illustration upside down and follow 1, 2, 3, 4, etc. Work each stitch in two separate movements — push the needle down through the canvas and gently pull the stitch into position. Then push the needle back up through the canvas and, again, pull the thread through into position ready for the next stitch.

The back of the work should show a long sloping stitch except when changing rows. This embroidery stitch should always be worked on a frame, otherwise it distorts the canvas badly and blocking may not correct the distortion.

Preparing a Hem with Mitred Corners

Tack guidelines (as indicated in diagram, Mitred Corner 1). The diagram shows a hem that is 10 threads wide. If your hem is to be 12 threads wide, intervals should be 12, 12 and 11 (instead of 10, 10 and 9). Cut off excess fabric along cutting line.

Mitred Corner 1

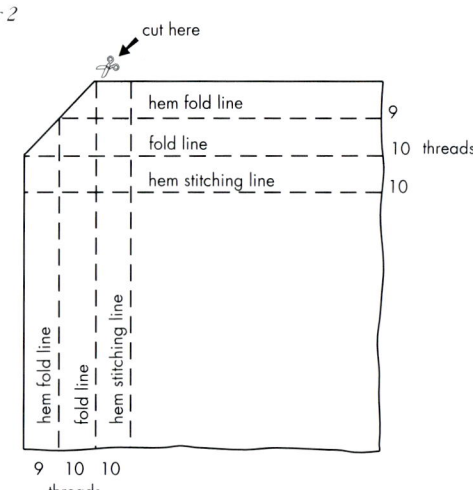

Cut angle for mitre using the tacking lines as a guide (see diagram, Mitred Corner 2).

Mitred Corner 2

Turn in the mitred edge (see diagram, Mitred Corner 3). Align tacking lines to ensure a perfect line. Pin.

Mitred Corner 3

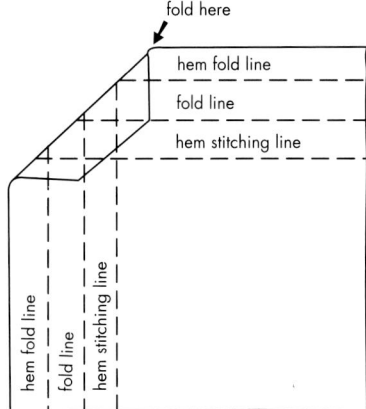

Turn in along hem fold line, turning mitred fold line at the same time (see diagram, Mitred Corner 4). Pin and tack.

Mitred Corner 4

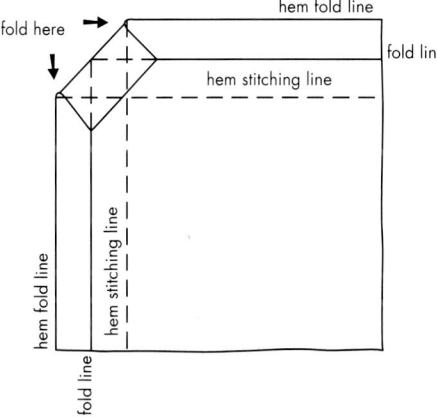

Turn in again along fold line (see diagram, Mitred Corner 5). Pin and tack, taking care that mitred edges meet.

Mitred Corner 5

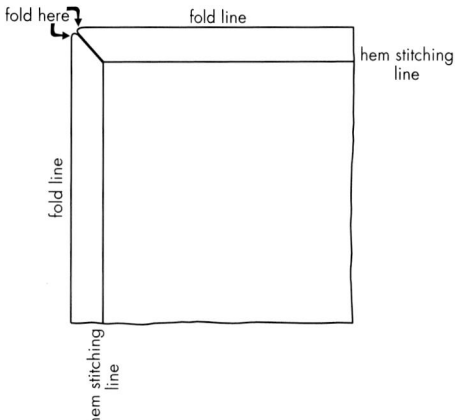

Slip stitch mitred corner with machine thread. Hem or Hem Stitch hem fold line to hem stitching line (see diagram, Mitred Corner 6).

Mitred Corner 6

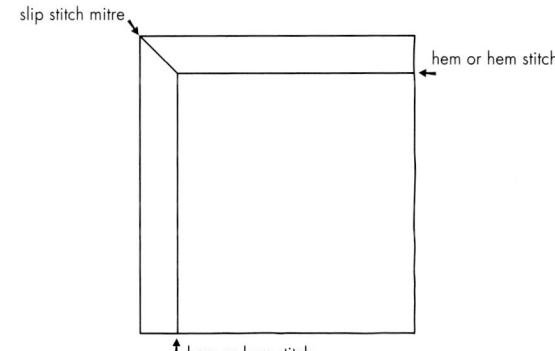

Assisi work supper cloth and serviette

Materials

SUPPER CLOTH

DMC Stranded Cotton (Art. 117) in the
following quantities and colours:
48 skeins 931
5 skeins 844
1 skein 300
Belfast Linen (Art. 3609–101) Antique
White, 1 square metre
Six tapestry needles, size 26 (see Hint,
below)
Machine thread in a medium colour and
ecru
Crewel needle, size 8 or 9
Embroidery scissors
Chart marker

FOR EACH SERVIETTE

DMC Stranded Cotton (Art. 117) in the
following quantities and colours:
2 skeins 931
2 metres 844
2 metres 300
Belfast Linen (Art. 3609–101) Antique
White, 40 × 40 cm
Machine thread in a medium colour and
ecru

Tapestry needles, size 26
Crewel needle, size 8 or 9
Embroidery scissors
Chart marker

Supper cloth

You may prefer to photocopy the charts
and tape them together before starting the
embroidery. The same border is worked on
all four sides of the cloth. Note that the
right-hand end of Chart 4 joins the top of
Chart 1, with the outermost rows matching
exactly and the Cross Stitch embroidery
continuing uninterrupted.

Zigzag by machine or oversew by hand
around all cut edges of the linen. Find the
centre of one side of the linen and tack a
line with the medium-coloured machine
thread across the linen from this point.
Measure 16 cm in from the outside of the
linen along the centre line. This point
corresponds with the top row of Cross Stitch
at the centre line marked on Chart 3. Start
the Cross Stitch here. Use two strands of
stranded cotton for the Cross Stitch. A chart
marker will be invaluable for keeping track

CHART 1

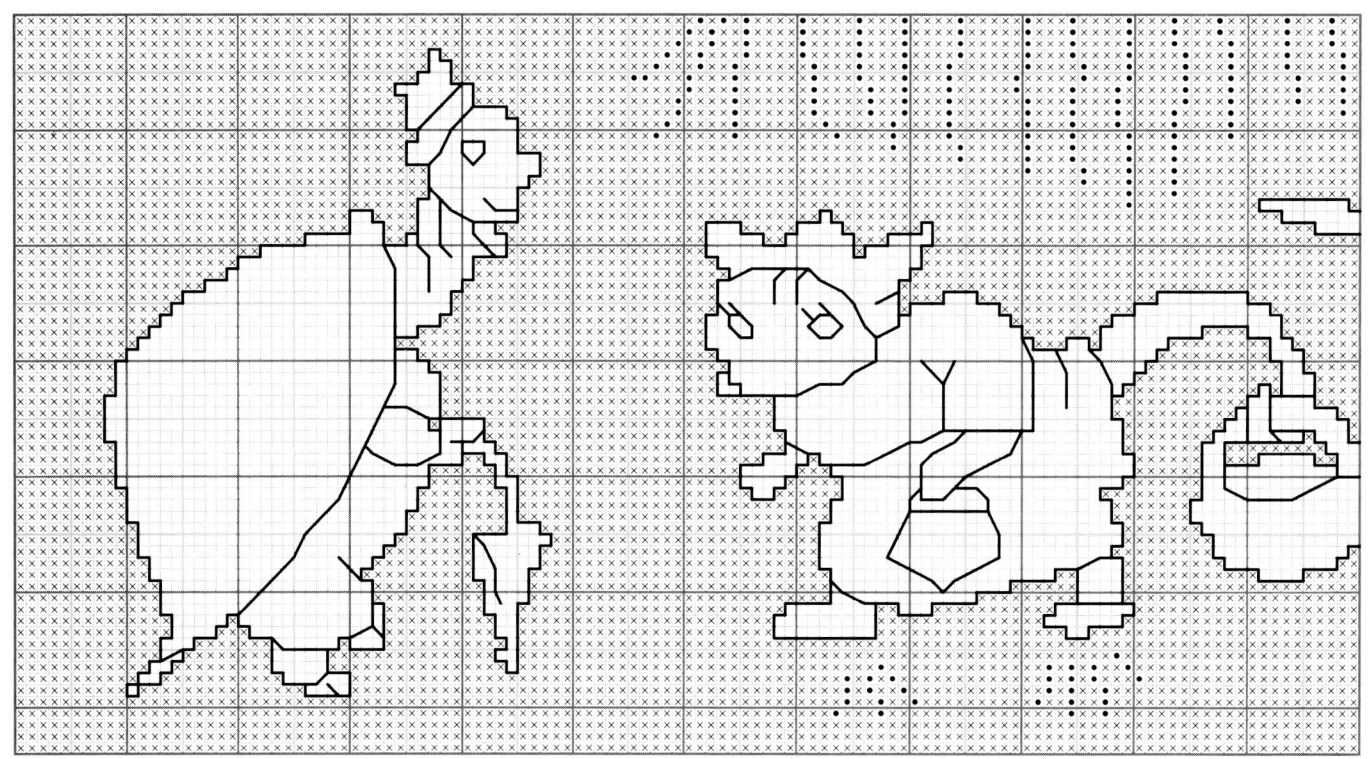

KEY
☒ 931 medium antique blue
▣ 844 ultra dark beaver grey
◡ 300 very dark mahogany

of the rows of Cross Stitch in this design. Instuctions for Cross Stitch are given on page 9.

Work the medium antique blue Cross Stitch first (see Hint, below), then the ultra dark medium grey Cross Stitch. Work the Double Running Stitch outlines last, using one strand of cotton.

When the embroidery is complete, press the linen on the wrong side and remove the tacked centre line.

Six threads from the edge of the embroidery, make a doubled hem 20 threads wide, mitring the corners (follow the instructions on pages 12-13). Hem the cloth with ecru machine thread in the crewel needle.

Remove all tacking lines and press the finished project on the wrong side of the work.

HINT: Thread six needles with medium antique blue stranded cotton and embroider these threads. Then stop, change your sitting position, re-thread the six needles and recommence your embroidery. This method is quicker and more comfortable when working large areas of one colour.

CHART 2

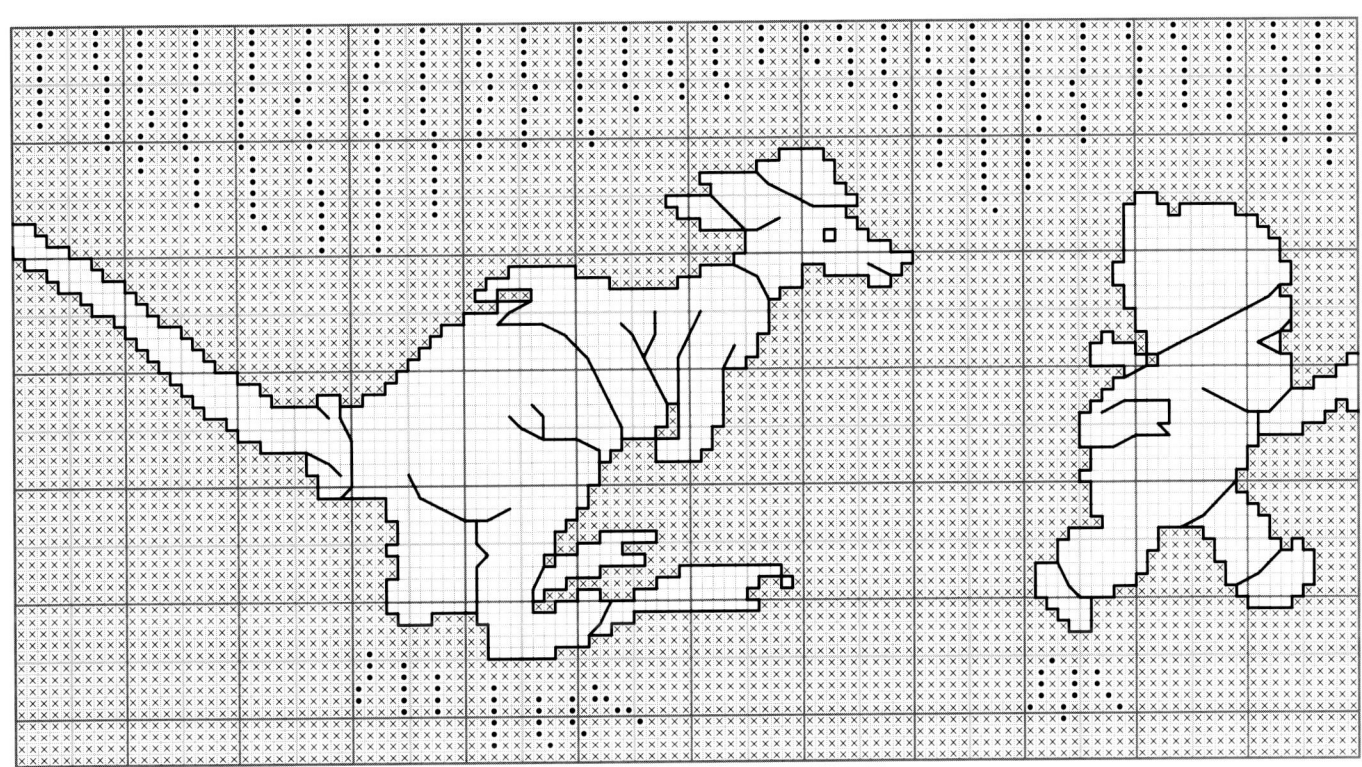

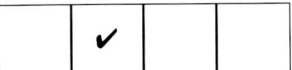

CHART 3

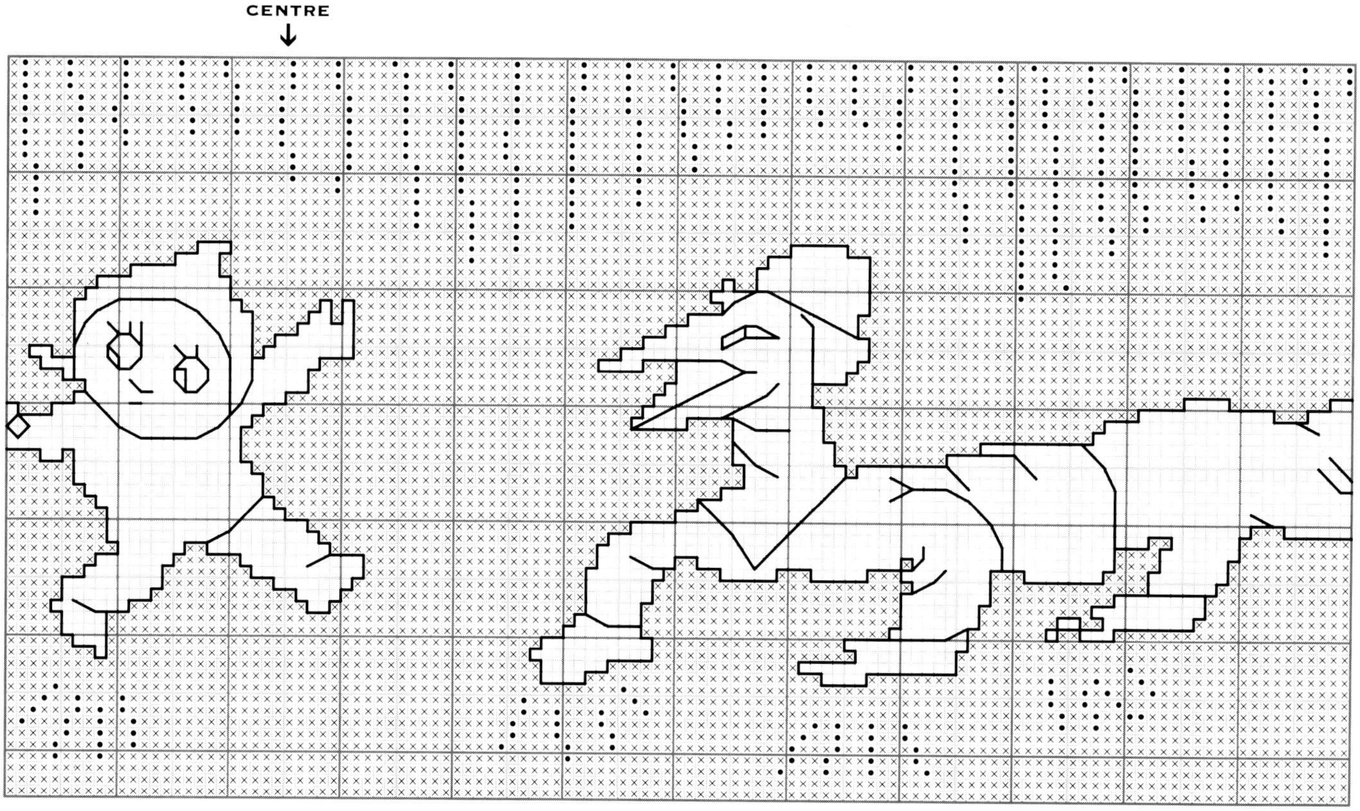

CENTRE

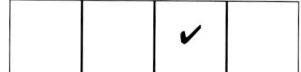

CHART 4

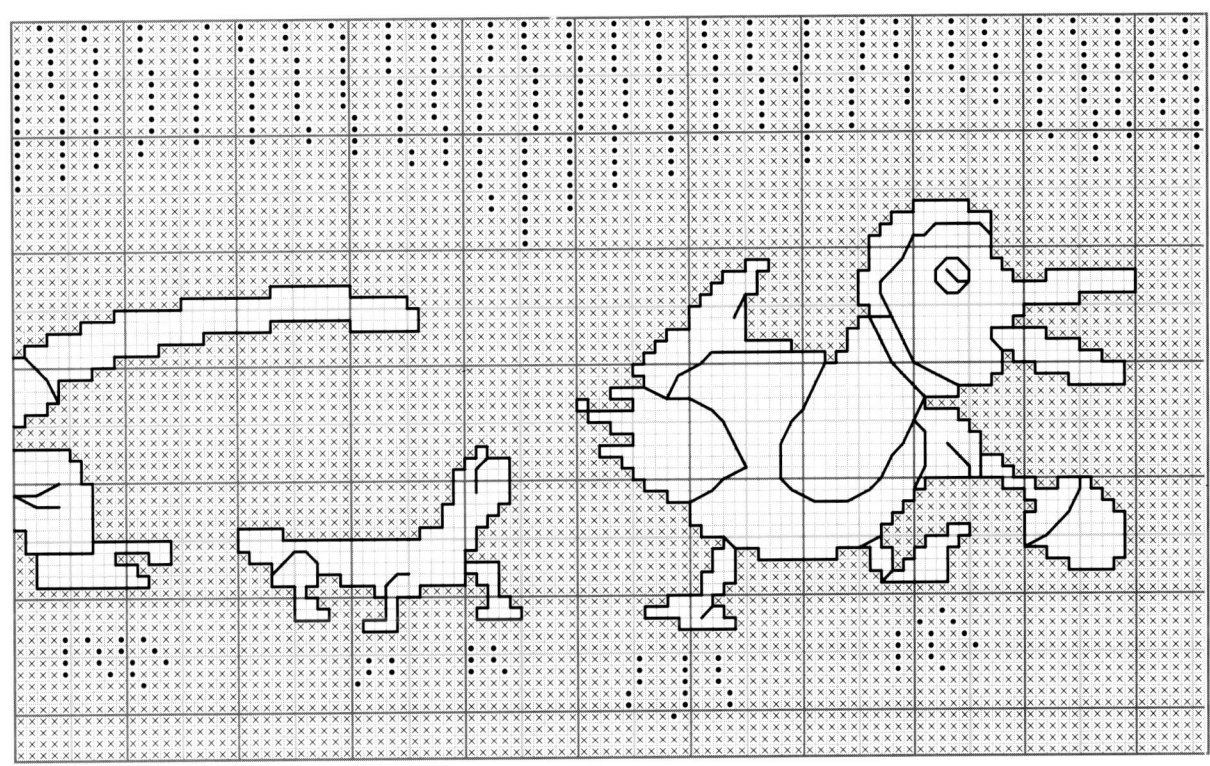

Serviette

Each serviette is the same. Zigzag by machine or oversew by hand around the cut edges of the linen. The embroidered motif is worked in the lower left-hand corner of the linen.

Measure 3 cm in from the left-hand edge of the linen, and 11 cm up from the bottom edge of the linen. This point corresponds with the top left-hand Cross Stitch on the Kookaburra, Chart 5. Start the embroidery here. Following the instructions for Cross Stitch on page 9, work the medium antique blue Cross Stitch first with two strands of cotton, then the ultra dark beaver grey Cross Stitch, and finally the Double Running Stitch with one strand of the very dark mahogany thread.

When the embroidery is complete, press it on the wrong side.

Four threads from the outer edge of the embroidered motif, make a doubled hem 10 threads wide, mitring the corners (follow the instructions on pages 12-13). Hem the serviettes with ecru machine thread in the crewel needle.

Remove all tacking lines and press the finished serviette on the wrong side.

CHART 5

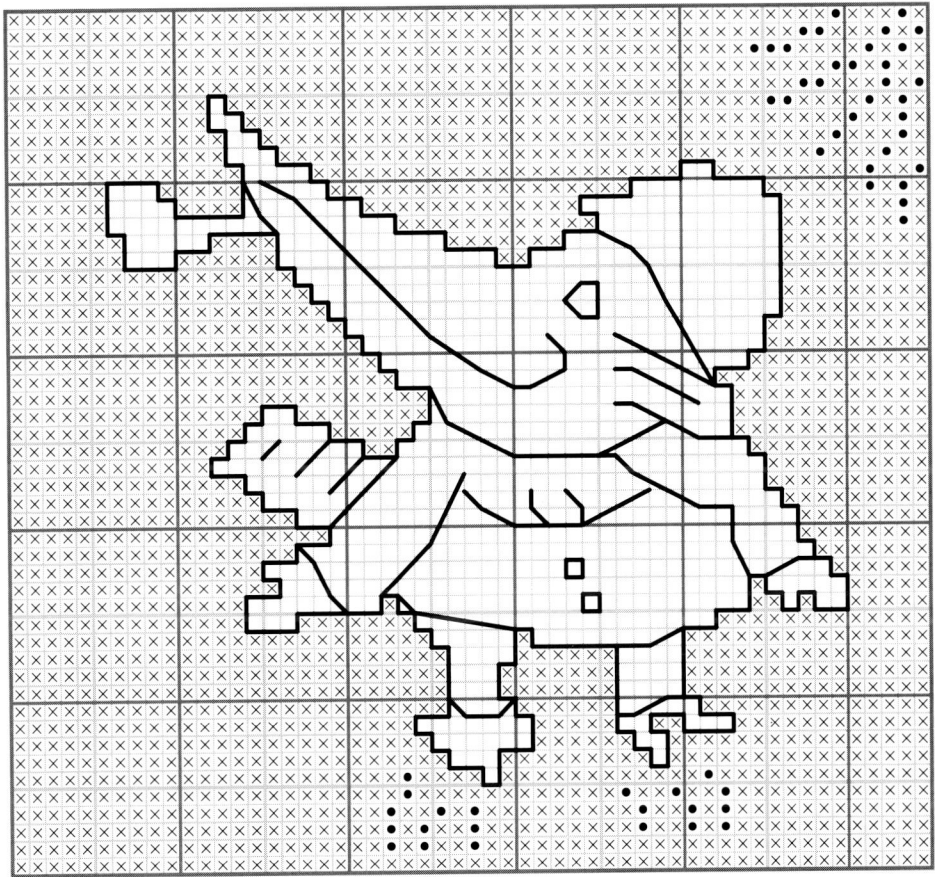

KEY

☒ 931 medium antique blue

⊙ 844 ultra dark beaver grey

╲ 300 very dark mahogany

Flowers by Lisa Milasas

Delphiniums placemat and serviette

Materials

FOR EACH PLACEMAT

DMC Stranded Cotton (Art. 117) in the
following quantities and colours:
1 skein 320
1 skein 340
1 skein 341
1 skein 367
1 skein 368
1 skein 677
1 skein 746
1 skein 799
1 skein 800
1 skein 809
1 skein 3042
1 skein 3747
Aida (Art. 3973–1) 18 count White,
58 × 43 cm
Machine thread in a medium colour
and white
Tapestry needle, size 26
Crewel needle, size 8 or 9
Embroidery scissors

FOR EACH SERVIETTE

DMC Stranded Cotton (Art. 117) in the
following quantities and colours (note
that this quantity of thread will be
sufficient for six serviettes):
1 skein 340
1 skein 341
1 skein 368
1 skein 677
1 skein 746
1 skein 799
1 skein 800
1 skein 809
1 skein 3747
Aida (Art. 3973–1) 18 count White,
43 × 43 cm (note that this quantity
of fabric will be sufficient for *one*
serviette).
Machine thread in a medium colour
and white
Tapestry needle, size 26
Crewel needle, size 8 or 9
Embroidery scissors

CHART 1

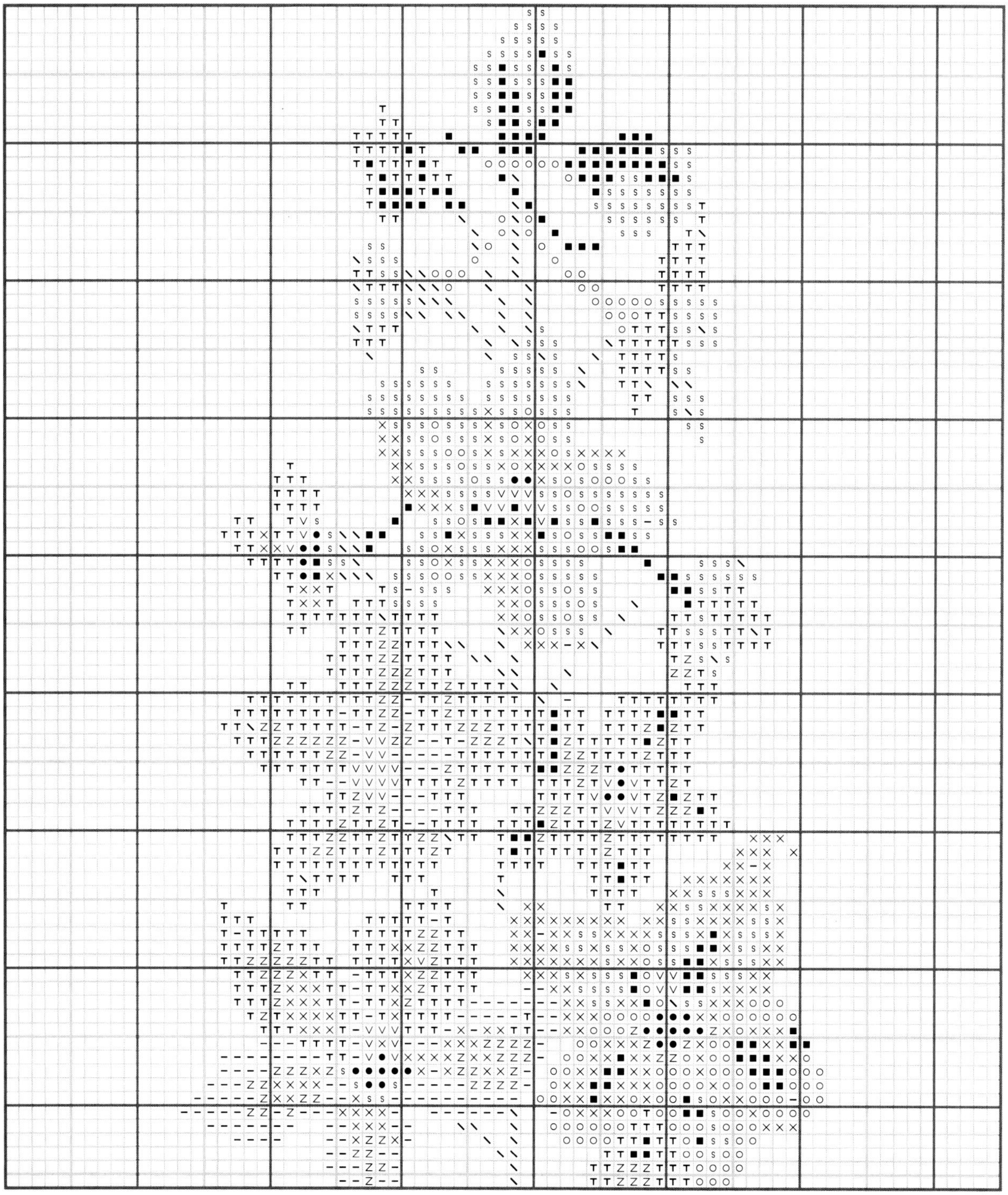

KEY

⊞	367 dark pistachio green		ℤ	809 delft
⧅	368 light pistachio green		−	799 medium delft
⬚	320 medium pistachio green		⑂	3747 very light blue violet
●	677 very light old gold		⊠	341 light blue violet
⋁	746 off white		○	340 medium blue violet
⊤	800 pale delft		■	3042 light antique violet

CHART 2

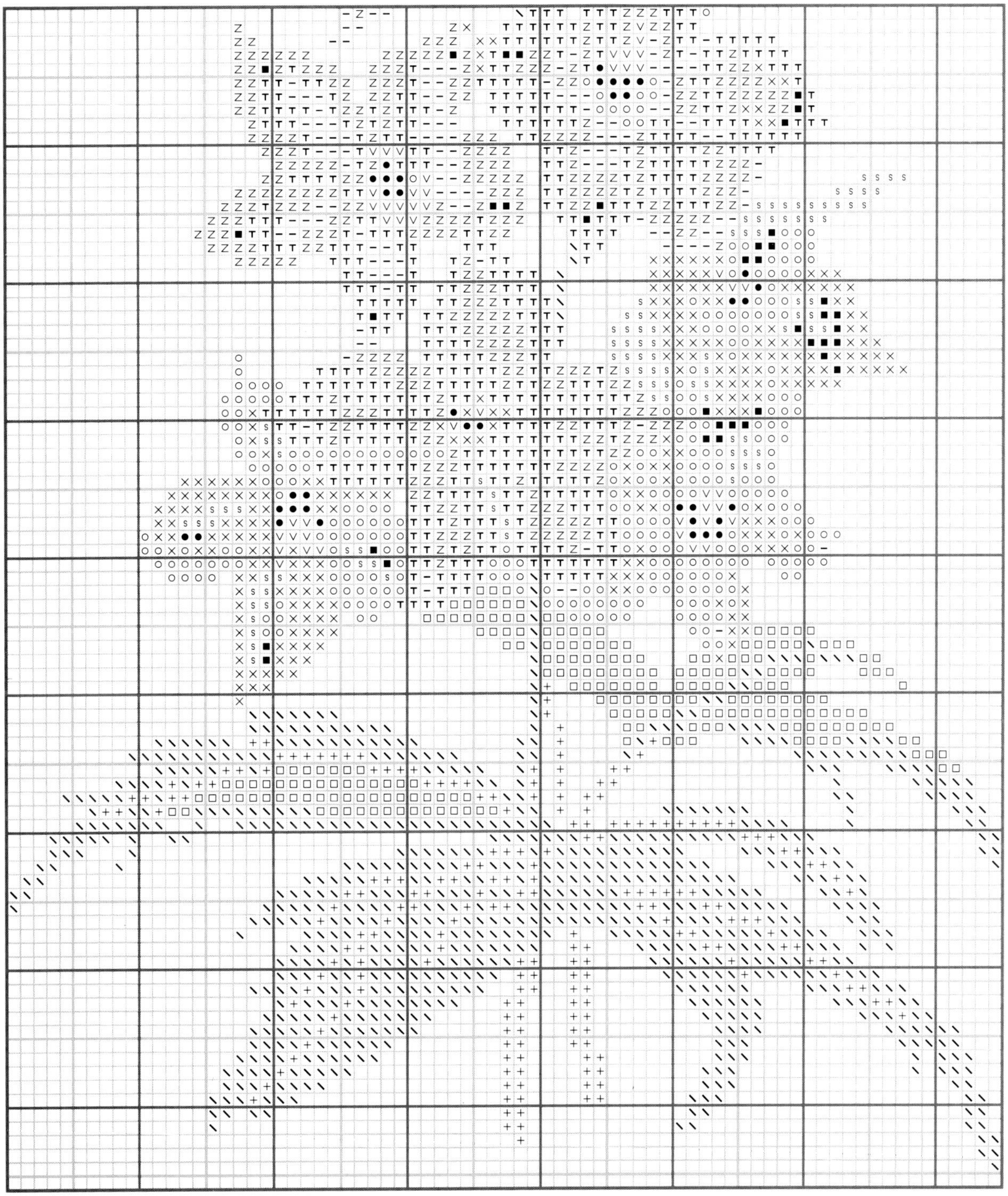

Placemat

Zigzag by machine or oversew by hand around the cut edges of each piece of Aida fabric.

Find the centre of one short side of the fabric and tack a line with the coloured machine thread across the placemat from this point.

Measure 13 cm in from the top left-hand corner along one long side of the fabric and tack a line with the coloured machine thread down the placemat.

The point where these two tacked lines cross corresponds with the centre stitch on the top row on Chart 2 of the Delphiniums design. Start the embroidery here, and work down the placemat, following the Cross Stitch instructions on page 9. Use two strands of embroidery cotton for the whole design.

After completing the lower half of the design, turn the chart for the top half of the design and the fabric around 180 degrees, and work the other half of the design. (The fabric and chart are turned upside down because it is much easier to work down a piece of Cross Stitch than it is to work up.)

The Hem Stitching line is 24 bundles to the left of the outermost stitch when counting along the tacked centre line. The Hem Stitching line at the right side of the placemat is 41 cm to the right of the left Hem Stitching line.

Make a double hem 6 bundles wide around the placemat, mitring the corners (follow the instructions on pages 12-13). Hem the placemat with white machine thread in the crewel needle.

Work a line of Back Stitch around the placemat 8 bundles inside the Hem Stitching line. Use one strand of 341 in the tapestry needle for the Back Stitch. Remove all tacking lines, and press the finished project on the wrong side.

Serviette

Zigzag by machine or oversew by hand around the cut edges of each piece of Aida fabric.

Tack one line 7.5 cm in from the raw edge of one side of the serviette, and another line 7.5 cm in from the raw edge of the adjacent side. The point at which these lines cross corresponds with the centre of Chart 3 of the Delphinium design. Start the Cross Stitch here. Use two strands of embroidery cotton.

When the embroidery is complete, remove the tacked centre lines. The Hem Stitching lines are 15 bundles down from the outermost stitches on the single delphinium motif. Hem as for placemat. Press the embroidery on the wrong side.

SERVIETTE

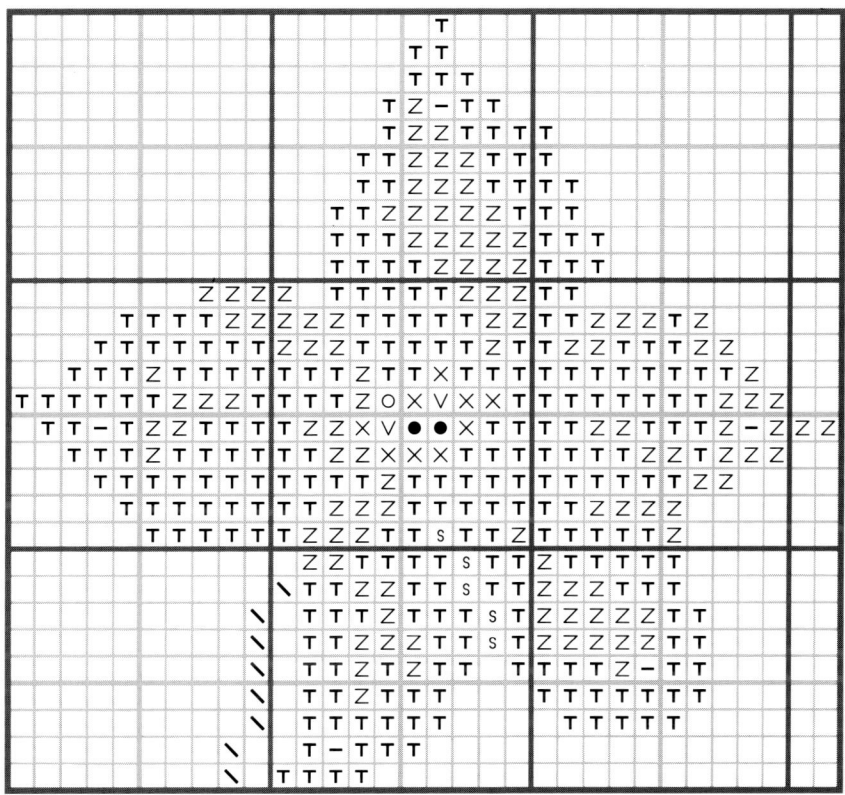

KEY

↘	368	light pistachio green
●	677	very light old gold
∨	746	off white
T	800	pale delft
Z	809	delft
−	799	medium delft
s	3747	very light blue violet
X	341	light blue violet
O	340	medium blue violet

Flowers by Lisa Milasas
Tray from Victoria's Old Charm Antiques

Gum Leaves black work traycloth

Materials

DMC Stranded Cotton (Art. 117) in the
   following quantity and colour:
   2 skeins 3345
Belfast Linen (Art. 3609–222) Cream
   colour, 60 × 47 cm
Machine thread in a medium colour
Tapestry needle, size 26
Embroidery scissors

Zigzag by machine or oversew by hand
around the cut edges of the linen.
Measure 7 cm in and down from the top
left-hand corner of the fabric. This point
corresponds with the top left of the design
on Chart 1 of the Gum Leaves charts. Start
the embroidery here. All the design is
worked in Double Running Stitch (see
instructions on page 10). Use two strands
of thread for all the embroidery.
When the embroidery is complete, press
the fabric on the wrong side.
Make a doubled hem 14 threads wide
around the tray cloth (see instructions on
pages 12-13). The Hem Stitching line is
10 threads outside the outermost Double
Running Stitches on all sides of the work.
Hem Stitch the hem using cream machine
thread, following the Hem Stitching
instructions on page 11.
Remove all tacking threads and press
the finished project on the wrong side of
the work.

CHART 1

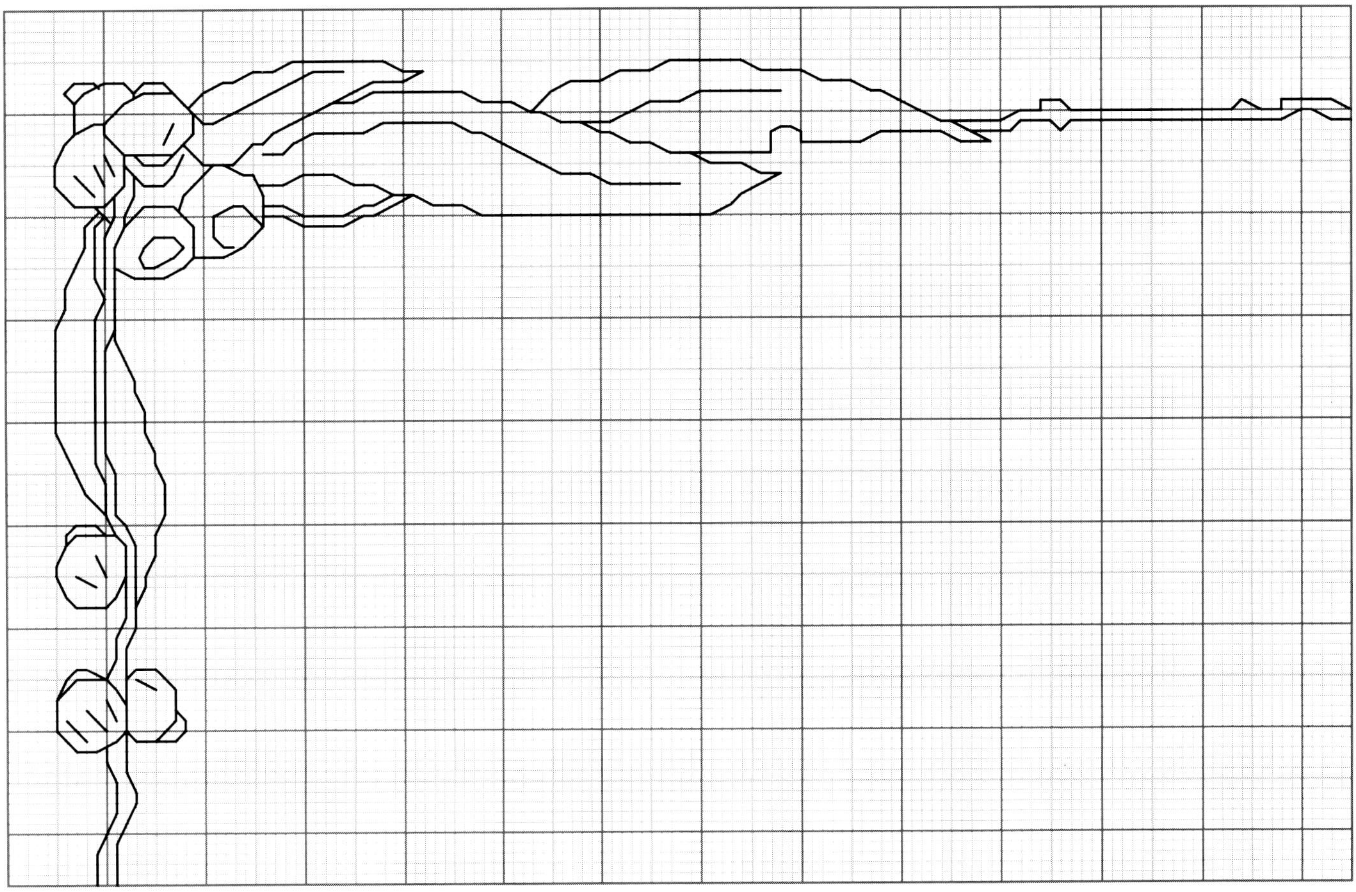

KEY

⌐ 3345 dark hunter green

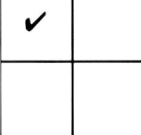

CHART 2

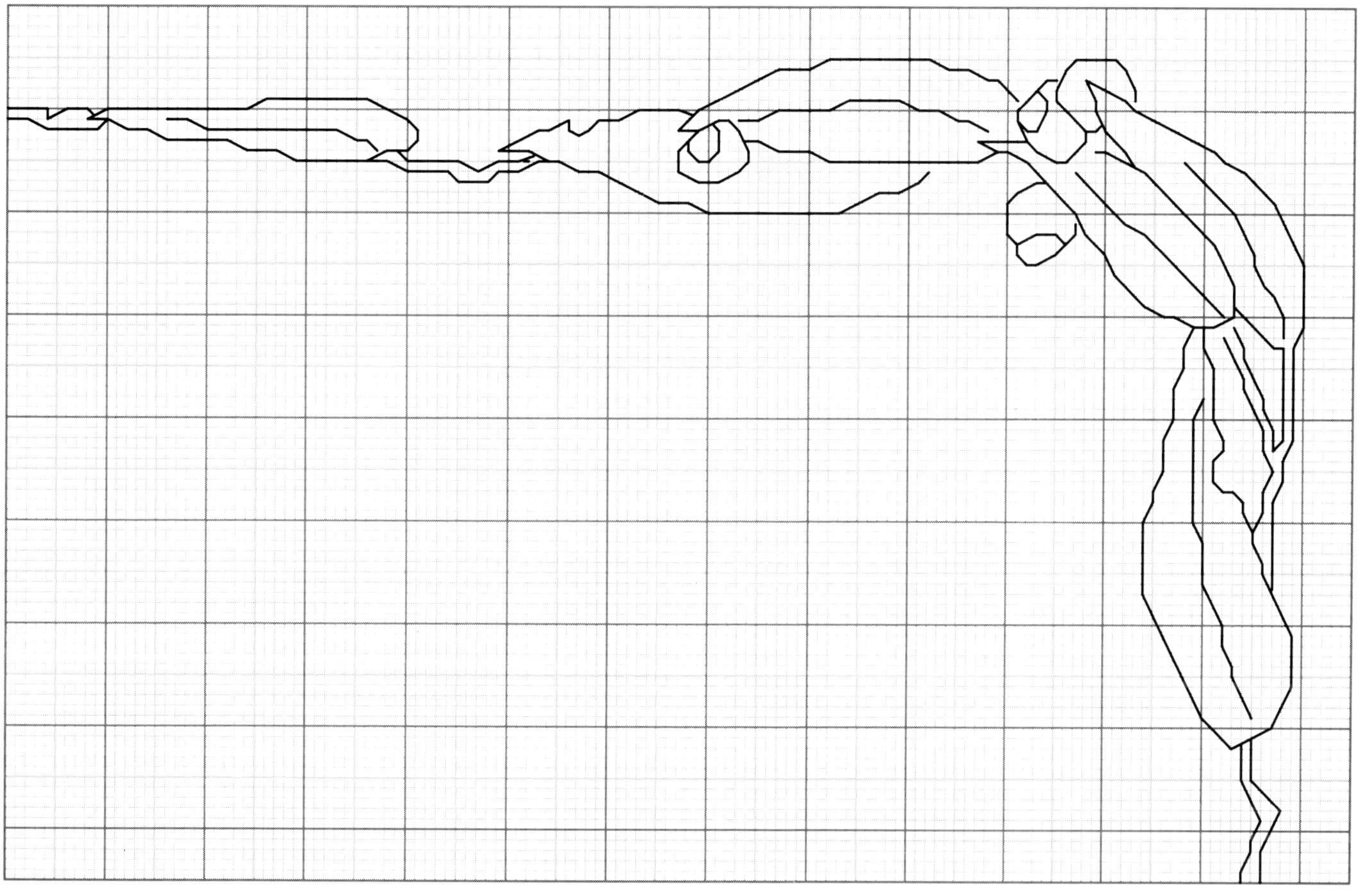

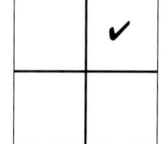

CHART 3

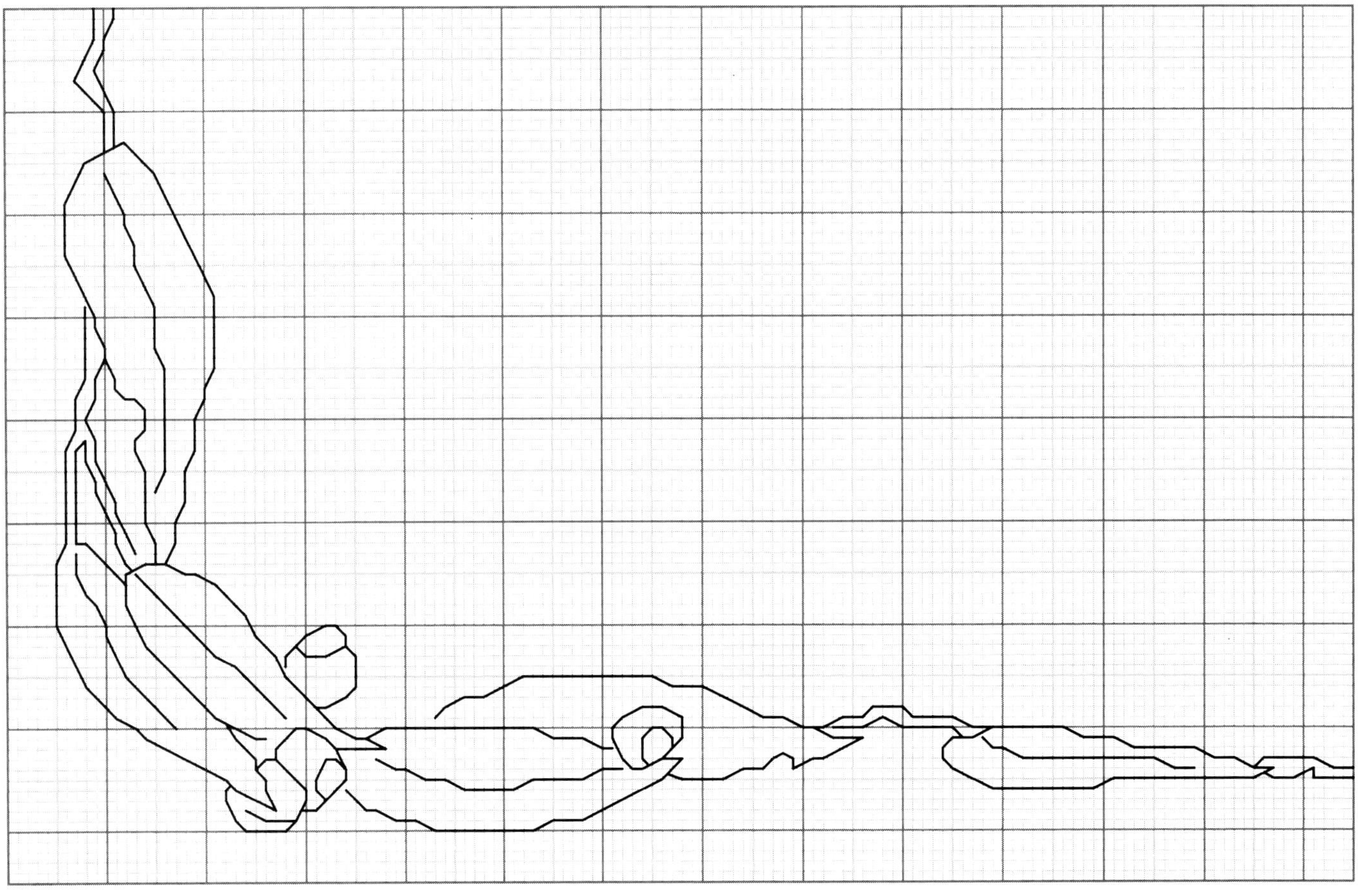

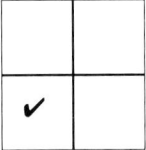

CHART 4

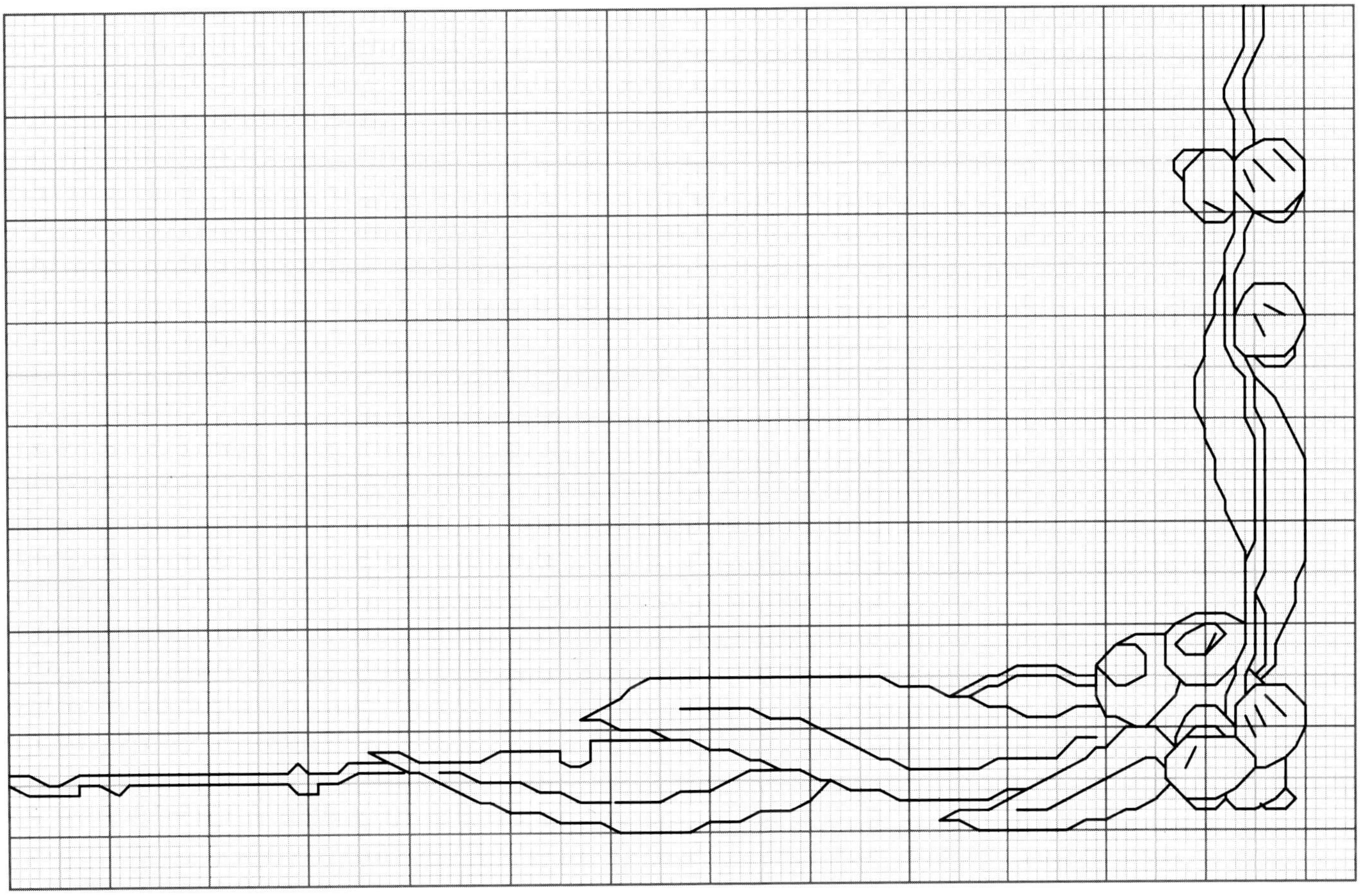

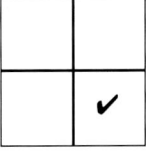

Flowers by Lisa Milasas

Christmas Bush handkerchief and sachet

Materials

HANDKERCHIEF

DMC Stranded Cotton (Art. 117) in the
following quantities and colours:
1 skein 351
1 skein 352
1 skein 677
1 skein 3052

DMC Linen Handkerchief (Art. D790)
with spoked edges

DMC Cordonnet Special (Art. 151–60)
Size 60 White, 1 ball

Crewel needle, size 9 or 10

Crochet hook, size 2 mm

Embroidery hoop, approximately 7 cm
diameter

Embroidery scissors

HB pencil

SACHET

DMC Stranded Cotton (Art. 117) in the
following quanitites and colours:
1 skein 350
1 skein 351
1 skein 352
1 skein 677

1 skein 3051
1 skein 3052

White organdie or organza, 30 cm

White machine thread

Crewel needle, size 9 or 10

Embroidery hoop, approximately 15 cm
diameter

Embroidery scissors

HB pencil

Handkerchief

Crochet edging

ROUND 1: Work 1 double crochet (dc) in
every hole around the handkerchief. Work
3 dc in each corner hole.

ROUND 2: *Chain (ch) 5, skip (sk) 3 dc, 1
treble (tr) in next dc**. Repeat * to ** for
full round. At corners 1 tr in last dc on side,
ch 7, 1 tr in 1st dc around corner.

ROUND 3: Work shell in every alternate
chain loop. Shell is made by (1 tr, ch 2, 1 tr,
ch 5, dc in 4th ch from hook, ch 2, 1 tr, ch 2,
1 tr) all in one chain loop. *Sk next chain
loop, shell in next chain loop**. Repeat *
to ** to complete round. Fasten off.

Dampen the edging. Stretch and pin to flat surface. Dry thoroughly.

Embroidery

Lightly trace the small Christmas Bush design onto one corner of the handkerchief approximately 2 cm in from the edge of the handkerchief. Use the sharp HB pencil and very light pressure.

Embroider the design in Shadow Work, following the stitch instructions on page 10. Use one strand of embroidery thread in the crewel needle.

When the embroidery is complete, press the handkerchief on the wrong side.

Sachet

Lightly trace the Christmas Bush design onto the organdie. Position the design in the middle of the fabric, about 12 cm in from the selvedge. Use the sharp HB pencil and very light pressure.

Embroider the Christmas Bush design with Shadow Work, following the stitch instructions on page 10. Use one strand of embroidery thread in the crewel needle. When the embroidery is complete, press the work on the wrong side.

Cut out the Sachet from the organdie as shown in the diagram. Work a French seam at the side seams and a small doubled hem around the flap and across the inside hem of the sachet.

SACHET

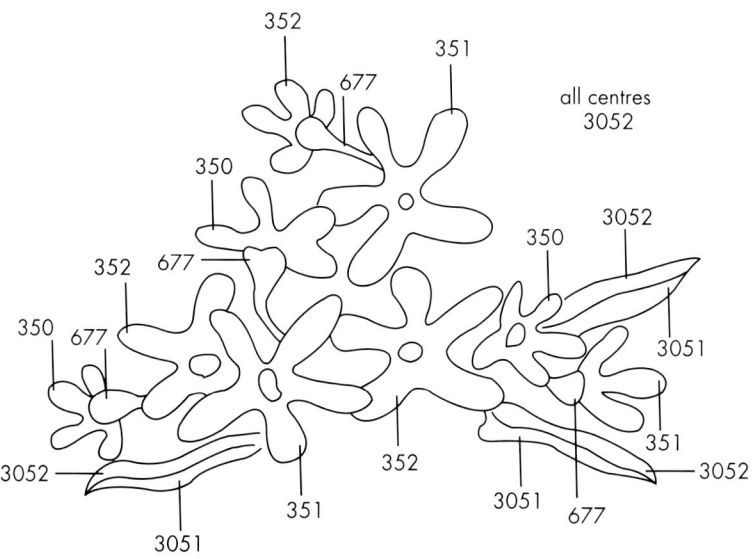

HANDKERCHIEF

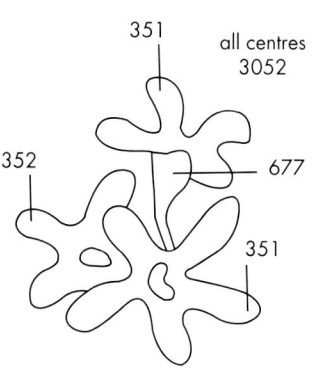

KEY

350 medium coral
351 coral
352 light coral
677 very light old gold
3051 dark green grey
3052 medium green grey

**CUTTING DIAGRAM
FOR SACHET**

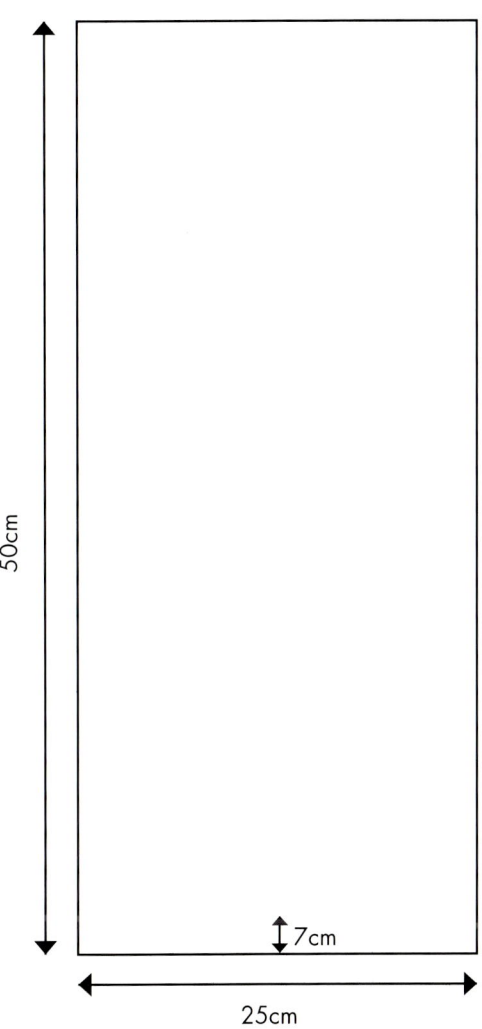

50cm

7cm

25cm

a.
es,

that

Cross Stitch bookmarks

Materials

FLANNEL FLOWER BABY

DMC Stranded Cotton (Art. 117) in the
 following quantities and colours:
 1 skein 712
 1 skein 761
 1 skein 927
 1 skein 3046
 1 skein 3047
 1 skein 3053
 1 skein 3328
 1 skein 3713
Sheet of perforated paper, ecru colour
Tapestry needle, size 24
Embroidery scissors

CHRISTMAS BELL BABY

DMC Stranded Cotton (Art. 117) in the
 following quantities and colours:
 1 skein 350
 1 skein 351
 1 skein 606
 1 skein 743
 1 skein 744
 1 skein 760
 1 skein 761
 1 skein 3713
Sheet of perforated paper, ecru colour
Tapestry needle, size 24
Embroidery scissors

NATIVE ROSE BABY

DMC Stranded Cotton (Art. 117) in the
 following quantities and colours:
 1 skein 347
 1 skein 758
 1 skein 890
 1 skein 987
 1 skein 3012
 1 skein 3013
 1 skein 3328
Sheet of perforated paper, ecru colour
Tapestry needle, size 24
Embroidery scissors

Flannel Flower Baby

Cut a piece of perforated paper 10 × 10 cm.
Measure 1.5 cm down from the top and
4 cm in from the right edge. Start the
embroidery here, at the top of the uppermost
petal of the flannel flower. Use four strands
of stranded cotton for the Cross Stitch, and
follow the stitch instructions on page 9.
When the Cross Stitch is complete, work
the Back Stitch details with two strands of
stranded cotton.
When the embroidery is complete, cut out
the embroidery from the perforated paper
leaving one row of paper around the design.

Christmas Bell Baby

Cut a piece of perforated paper 8 × 13 cm. Measure 1.5 cm down from the top and 2.5 cm in from the right edge. Start the embroidery here, at the top of the stem on the flower. Use four strands of stranded cotton for the Cross Stitch, and follow the stitch instructions on page 9.

When the embroidery is complete, cut out the embroidery from the perforated paper leaving one row of paper around the design.

Native Rose Baby

Cut a piece of perforated paper 8 × 14 cm. Measure 1.5 cm down from the top of the paper. Start the Cross Stitch at the top of the design. Use four strands of stranded cotton for the Cross Stitch, and follow the stitch instructions on page 9.

When the Cross Stitch is complete, work the Back Stitch details with 2 strands of stranded cotton.

When the embroidery is complete, cut out the embroidery from the perforated paper leaving one row of paper around the design.

Tassels

Make a tassel for each bookmark in the following colours:

Native Rose Baby: 987
Christmas Bell Baby: 351
Flannel Flower Baby: 712

Use the full thickness of the stranded cotton for the tassel. Cut two 20 cm lengths of stranded cotton and a 5 cm square of cardboard.

Place one 20 cm length of cotton along the cardboard. Using the skein of cotton, wind cotton around the cardboard 25 times, finishing at the same side you started. Tightly tie together the ends of the 20 cm thread that is inside the wound cotton. Slide the cardboard out of the bundle of threads. Bind the neck of the tassel about 1 cm from the top with the second 20 cm length of thread. Securely tie together the ends of the binding thread. One at a time, thread the ends of the binding thread through a needle and pass the needle behind the binding, pulling it out to become part of the skirt of the tassel.

Cut the loops at the bottom of the skirt. Trim ends evenly. Plait the ends of the first thread (at the top of the tassel) for 1 cm, then tie the ends together. Thread the ends through a needle and pass them through a hole in the Cross Stitch near the end of the embroidery. Tie the ends in a knot at the back of the embroidery. End off in the back of the embroidery to neaten.

FLANNEL FLOWER BABY

KEY

☐	3053	green grey
◥	712	cream
L	3047	light yellow beige
H	3046	medium yellow beige
Z	927	light grey green
■	3328	dark salmon
S	3713	very light salmon
T	761	light salmon

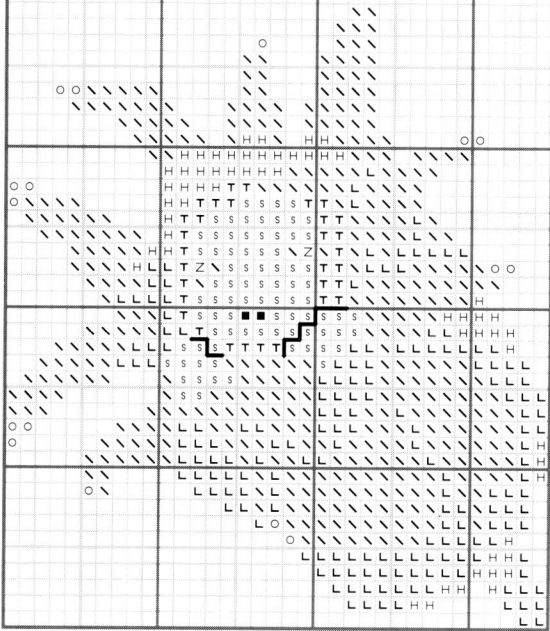

CHRISTMAS BELL BABY

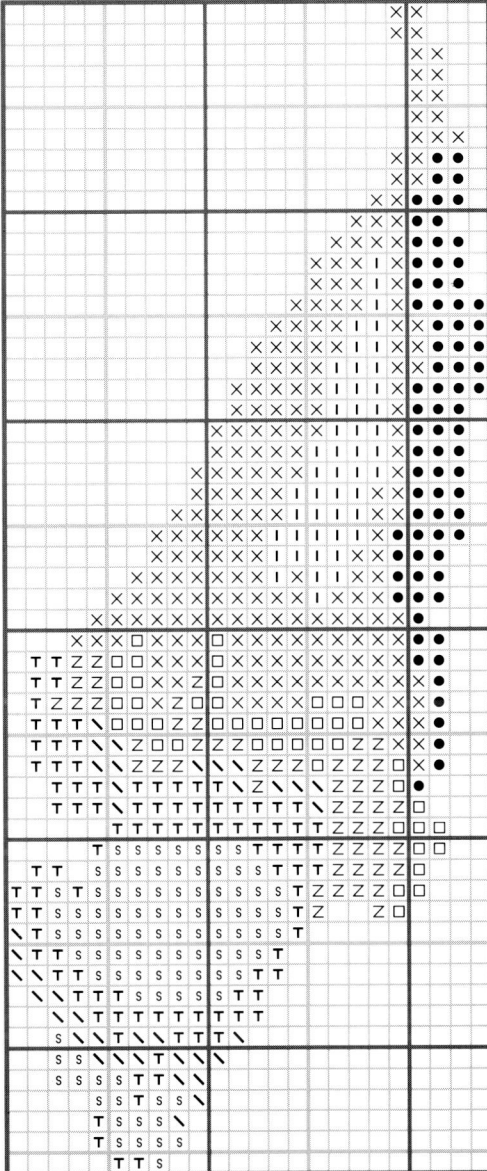

NATIVE ROSE BABY

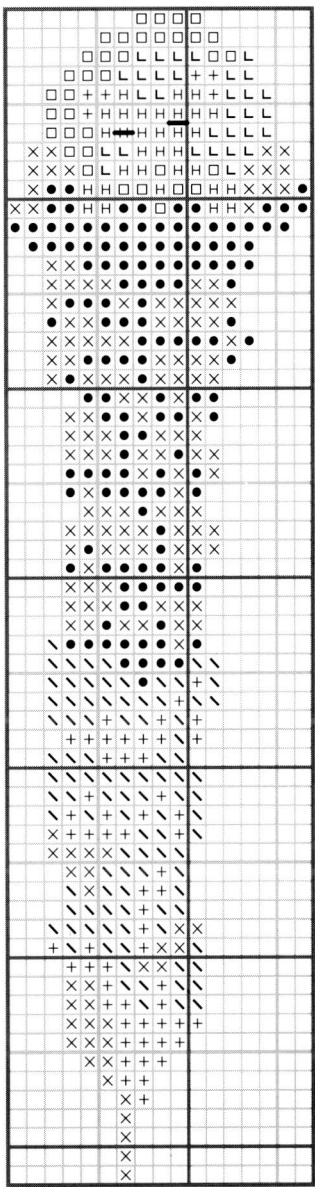

KEY

- ● 606 bright orange red
- I 350 medium coral
- ✗ 351 coral
- Z 743 medium yellow
- □ 744 pale yellow
- S 3713 very light salmon
- T 761 light salmon
- ＼ 760 salmon

KEY

- ● 890 ultra dark pistachio green
- ✗ 987 dark forest green
- ＋ 3012 medium khaki green
- ＼ 3013 light khaki green
- □ 347 very dark salmon pink
- L 3328 dark salmon
- H 758 very light terracotta

Cross Stitch greeting cards

Materials

FLANNEL FLOWER

DMC Stranded Cotton (Art. 117) in the
following quantities and colours:
1 skein ecru
1 skein 543
1 skein 680
1 skein 760
1 skein 761
1 skein 833
1 skein 926
1 skein 3047
1 skein 3053
1 skein 3348
1 skein 3713
Belfast Linen (Art. 3609–101) Antique
White, 15 × 11 cm (note that this
quantity of fabric will be sufficient for
one card)
Machine thread in a medium colour
Tapestry needle, size 26
Embroidery scissors
Greeting card with a window cut in the
centre to display embroidery
Stanfords 450 glue

GUM LEAF

DMC Stranded Cotton (Art. 117) in the
following quantities and colours:
1 skein 320
1 skein 368
1 skein 520
1 skein 522
1 skein 920
1 skein 922
Belfast Linen (Art. 3609–101) Antique
White, 15 × 11 cm (note that this
quantity of fabric will be sufficient for
one card)
Machine thread in a medium colour
Tapestry needle, size 26
Embroidery scissors
Greeting card with a window cut in the
centre to display embroidery
Stanfords 450 glue

CHRISTMAS BUSH

DMC Stranded Cotton (Art. 117) in the
following quantities and colours:
1 skein 350
1 skein 351
1 skein 352
1 skein 677
1 skein 3051
1 skein 3052
Belfast Linen (Art. 3609–101) Antique
White, 15 × 11 cm (note that this
quantity of fabric will be sufficient for
one card)
Machine thread in a medium colour
Tapestry needle, size 26
Embroidery scissors

Greeting card with a window cut in the
centre to display embroidery
Stanfords 450 glue

MAIDENHAIR FERN

DMC Stranded Cotton (Art. 117) in the
following quantity and colour:
1 skein 471
Belfast Linen (Art. 3609–101) Antique
White, 15 × 11 cm (note that this
quantity of fabric will be sufficient for
one card)
Machine thread in a medium colour
Tapestry needle, size 26
Embroidery scissors
Greeting card with a window cut in the
centre to display embroidery
Stanfords 450 glue

Zigzag by machine or oversew by hand

around the cut edges of the linen. Find the
centre of the linen and tack centre lines
each way across the linen. Find the centre
of the chart.
Start the embroidery in the centre. Work
the Cross Stitch and the Back Stitch with
two strands of stranded cotton, following
the stitch instructions on pages 9 and 12.
When the embroidery is complete, remove
the tacking lines and press the fabric on
the wrong side. Carefully place the
embroidery into the window of the
greeting card and centre the design in the
cut out window. Trim the linen to fit if
necessary. Place a little glue on the linen
outside the area to be seen through the
window and glue the linen in position.
Glue the return on the card in place to
hide the back of the embroidery.

FLANNEL FLOWER

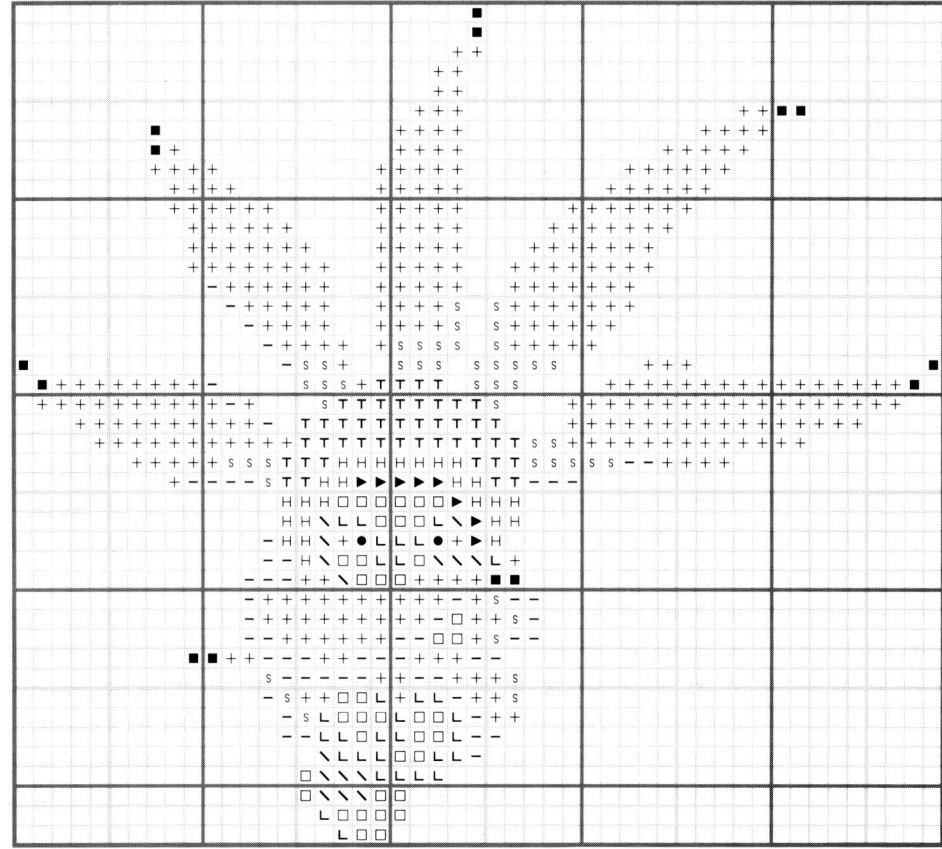

KEY

■ 3053 green grey	⊤ 3348 light yellow green	◥ 760 salmon	
ⓢ 3047 light yellow beige	⌖ 833 light golden olive	∟ 761 light salmon	
⊟ 543 ultra very light beige brown	▶ 680 dark old gold	☐ 3713 very light salmon	
⊞ ecru	● 926 medium grey green		

GUM LEAF

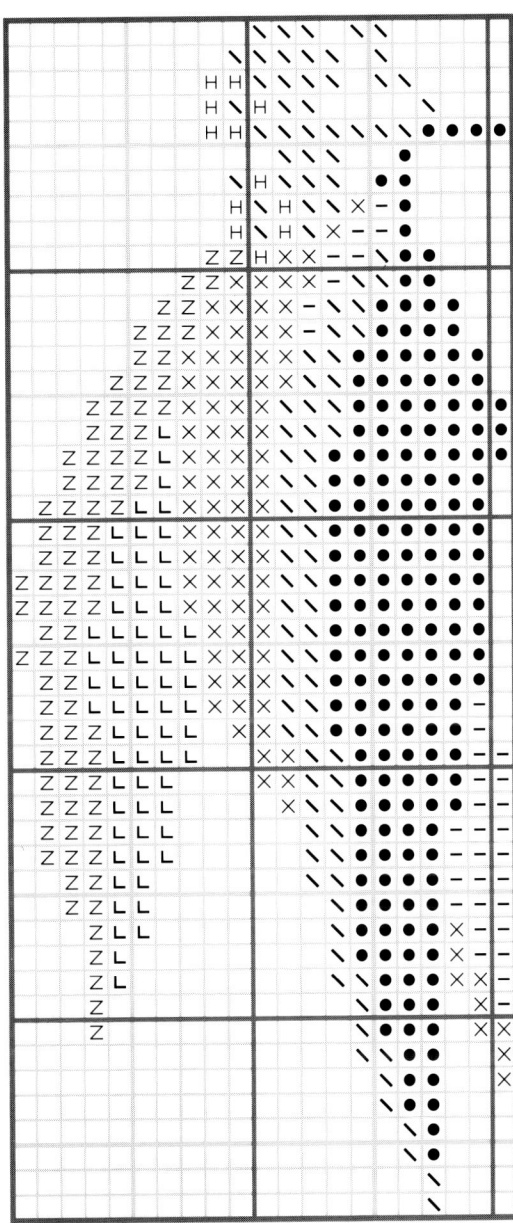

KEY

◥	920	medium copper
●	922	light copper
⊠	520	dark fern green
⊟	522	fern green
Z	320	medium pistachio green
L	368	light pistachio green

CHRISTMAS BUSH

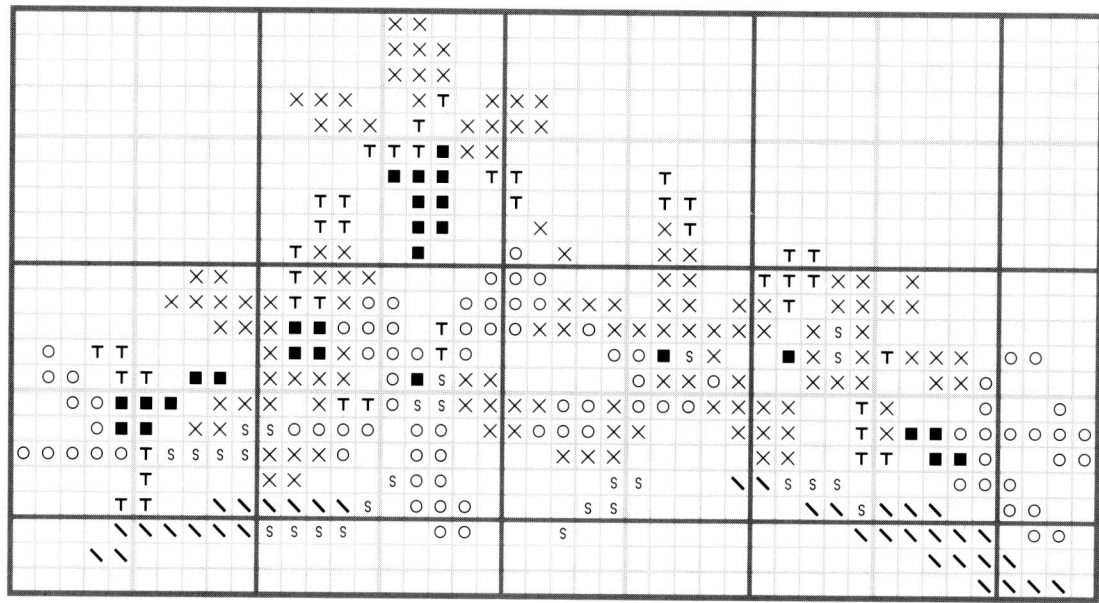

KEY

- T 350 medium coral
- ☒ 351 coral
- ☉ 352 light coral
- ╲ 3052 medium green grey
- ⓢ 3051 dark green grey
- ■ 677 very light old gold

MAIDENHAIR FERN

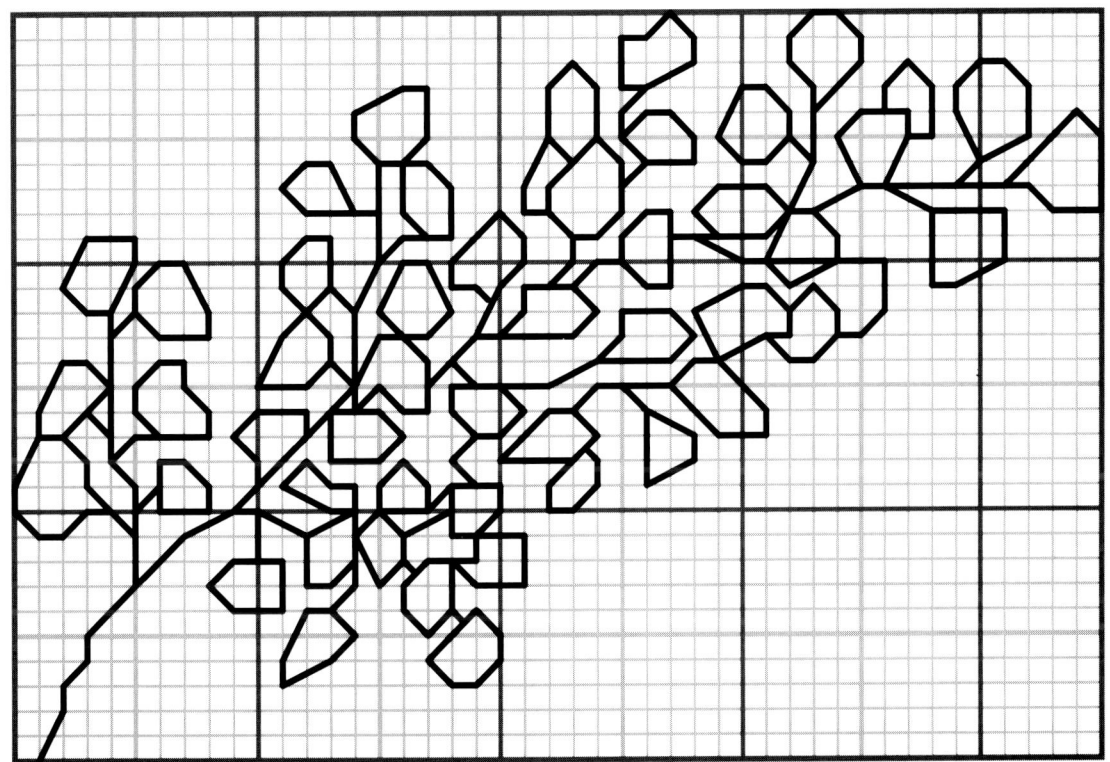

KEY

⌐ 471 very light avocado green

Flowers by Lisa Milasas

Pink Boronia bowl and linen collar

Materials

COLLAR

DMC Stranded Cotton (Art. 117) in the
  following quantities and colours:
  1 skein 725
  1 skein 761
  1 skein 819
  1 skein 3053
  1 skein 3348
  1 skein 3713
Medium-weight linen, white, 60 cm
Waste canvas, 14 stitches per inch, 30 × 30 cm
Machine thread in white and a medium
  colour
Crewel needle, size 8
Embroidery scissors
Small white button
Tracing paper
Water spray

BOWL

DMC Stranded Cotton (Art. 117) in the
  following quantities and colours:
  1 skein 725
  1 skein 761
  1 skein 819
  1 skein 3053
  1 skein 3348
  1 skein 3713
Damask Aida (Art.3229–1) 14 count White,
  18 × 18 cm
Machine thread in a medium colour
Tapestry needle, size 24
Embroidery scissors
Framecraft 4 inch diameter Porcelain Bowl
  (FPL5-SP) soft pink colour

Collar

Trace the collar pattern from page 53 onto
the tracing paper, taking care to trace the
cutting, stitching and grain lines.

Pin the collar pattern to a single thickness
of the white linen fabric, making sure that
the grain line on the pattern matches the
straight grain on the fabric.

Carefully tack the cutting and stitching
lines from the pattern, taking care *not* to
tack the pattern piece to the fabric. Unpin
the pattern piece as you go.

Turn the pattern piece over, and pin it to
the fabric a little distance from the first

tacked shape, taking care to match the grain. Again, tack the cutting and stitching lines to the fabric, taking care *not* to tack the pattern piece to the fabric. You should now have two tacked shapes on the linen. Cut the waste canvas into six equal-sized pieces. Pin three pieces onto each collar shape within the tacked stitching lines. Arrange the pieces attractively on the collar. The waste canvas and the linen do not have to have their grain lines matching, but the position of the pieces should be balanced.

Tack the canvas into position. If the waste canvas overlaps, make a note of the positions and tack one piece on and embroider the Boronia flowers one at a time. Note that there are three motifs for the left side of the collar, and three motifs (mirror-images of the first three) for the right side of the collar.

Embroider the flowers using Cross Stitch (follow the stitch instructions on page 9), stitching through the large holes on the waste canvas and the linen below. Use two strands of stranded cotton in the crewel needle. While working the Cross Stitch take care not to pierce the threads in the waste canvas.

When the motif is complete, spray the embroidery with cold water. Carefully remove the threads from the waste canvas, leaving the Cross Stitch on the linen. (Note: a pair of tweezers may be useful to remove the threads from the waste canvas.) Position the remaining pieces of waste canvas on the collar in the positions marked, and embroider the other Boronia motifs. Remove the waste canvas in the manner described above. Cut out the embroidered collar sections from the linen, along the cutting line tacked onto the fabric.

Cut one pair of collar sections from the remaining white linen fabric, using the collar pattern (page 53).

Trace the collar facing pattern piece (page 52) onto the tracing paper. Placing the pattern on the fold as indicated, cut two collar facing sections from the remaining white linen fabric.

Place each of the embroidered sections on one of a pair of the plain collar sections with right sides facing. Pin them together and machine stitch, following the stitching lines around the outer edge of the collar only. Grade and clip the curves around the seam allowances. Turn the collar sections right sides out and tack the raw edges together.

Pin the tacked sides of the embroidered collar sections onto one collar facing piece, matching the notches, and checking that the fronts of the embroidered pieces of the collar are close together. Pin the other collar facing piece onto the pinned section so that the embroidered pieces are sandwiched between the two facings. Stitch the notched seam. Grade and clip seam allowances. Turn collar facing right side out. Turn in lower edges of the collar facing, and hand or machine edges closed. Sew the button onto one side of the collar at the back and work a loop on the opposite side of the collar to fit.

Wear the collar with the facing inside a jumper, and the embroidered collar sitting neatly around the neck.

Bowl

Zigzag by machine or oversew by hand around all cut edges of the Aida fabric. Fold the fabric in half both ways and tack centre lines across the Aida. Find the centre of the chart. The centres of the chart and the Aida correspond. Start the Cross Stitch embroidery here, following the Cross Stitch instructions on page 9. Use two strands of cotton for the embroidery. When the Cross Stitch is complete, remove the tacking lines. Press the embroidery on the wrong side.

Mount the embroidery into the lid of the porcelain bowl, following the manufacturer's instructions.

COLLAR

BOWL

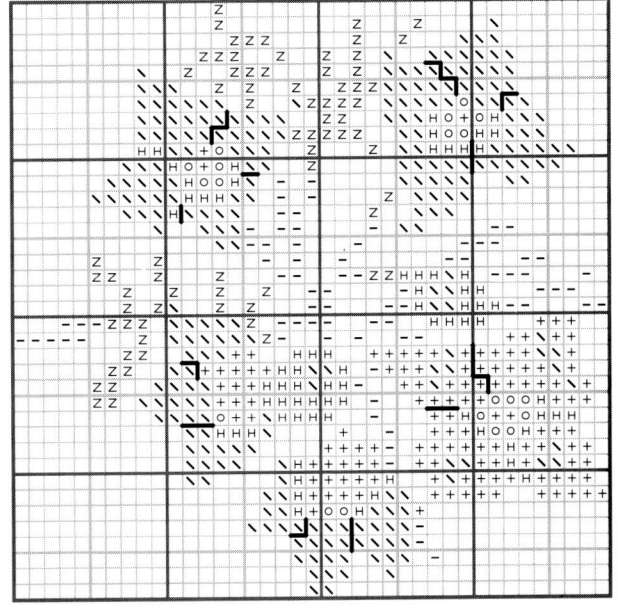

KEY

⊙	725	topaz
☑	3348	light yellow green
⊟	3053	green grey
⊞	761	light salmon
◥	3713	very light salmon
⊞	819	light baby pink

fold

straight of grain

COLLAR FACING

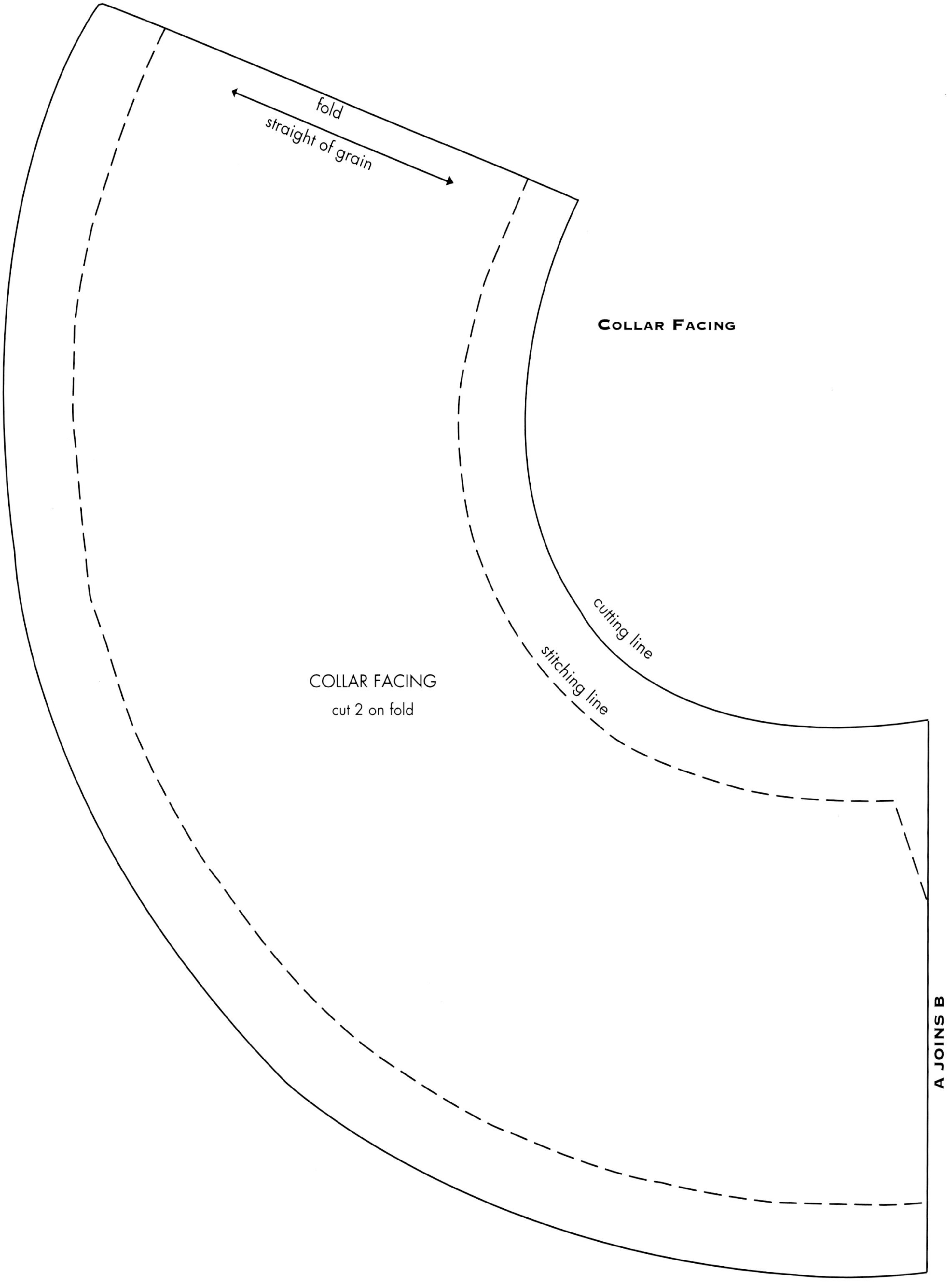

COLLAR FACING

cut 2 on fold

cutting line

stitching line

A JOINS B

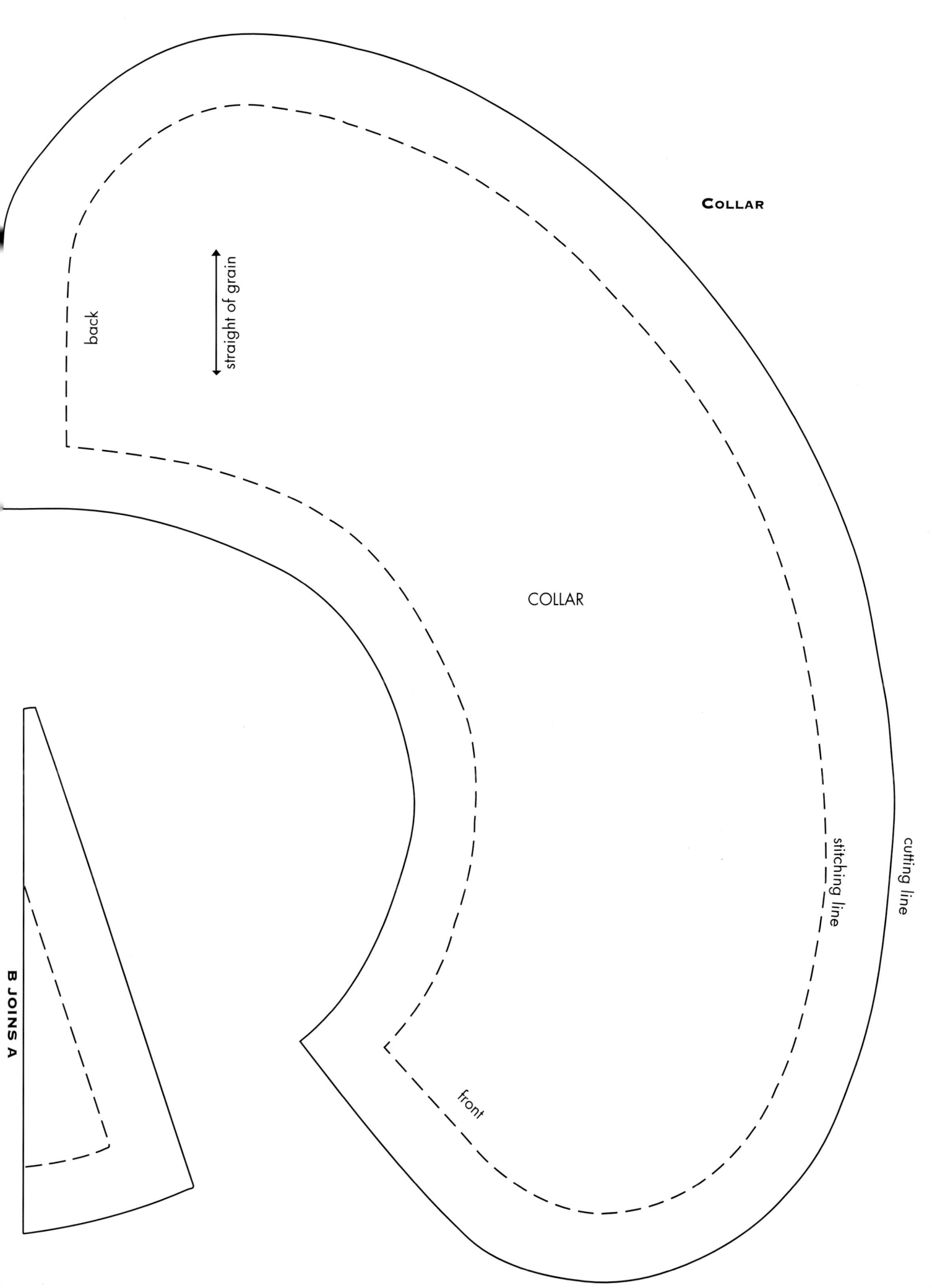

COLLAR

straight of grain

back

COLLAR

stitching line

cutting line

front

B JOINS A

Wattle towel set

Materials

BATH TOWEL

DMC Stranded Cotton (Art. 117) in the
  following quantities and colours:
  1 skein 320
  1 skein 725
  1 skein 744
  1 skein 3011
  1 skein 3348
Aida Band (Art. 7101–1) 14 count White,
  1 metre
White bath towel, approximately 73 × 136 cm
Machine thread, white
Tapestry needle, size 24
Crewel needle, size 8 or 9

HAND TOWEL

DMC Stranded Cotton (Art. 117) in the
  following quantities and colours:
  1 skein 320
  1 skein 725
  1 skein 744
  1 skein 3011
  1 skein 3348
Aida Band (Art. 7101–1) 14 count White,
  50 cm
Machine thread, white
White hand towel, approximately 36 × 64 cm
Tapestry needle, size 24
Crewel needle, size 8 or 9

Oversew by hand or zigzag by machine along cut edges of the Aida band. Count 30 bundles of threads in from the right-hand end of the Aida band. This point corresponds with the right-hand stitches of the Wattle Chart. Centre the design onto the Aida band and work the first Wattle motif in Cross Stitch, following the instructions on page 9. Use two strands of stranded cotton for the Cross Stitch. Leave 30 unworked bundles of threads between each Wattle motif. The bath towel will have six motifs embroidered across it and the hand towel will have three. The spacing is the same on both projects. When the Cross Stitch is complete, press the Aida band on the wrong side. Pin the Aida band onto the towel to cover the woven band in the towel, centring the embroidery across the towel and turning under the oversewn edges of the fabric. Slip stitch the Aida band onto the towel by hand, using the white machine thread in the crewel needle.

KEY

- ⊠ 725 topaz
- ⊡ 744 pale yellow
- Ⓛ 320 medium pistachio green
- Ⓣ 3348 light yellow green
- Ⓤ 3011 dark khaki green

Gum Leaf buttons

Materials

DMC Fil Or (Art. 284) gold thread, 1 reel
Damask Aida (Art. 3229–95) 14 count
  Black, four 8 × 8 cm squares
Tapestry needle
Self-cover buttons, four, 29 mm diameter
Embroidery scissors

Work the Gum Leaf design into the centre
of each square of black Aida fabric. Use
the full thickness of the gold thread for the
Double Running Stitch, and follow the
stitch instructions on page 10.

When the embroidery is complete, press
the fabric on the wrong side.
Make up the buttons following the
manufacturer's instructions.

NOTE: A row of fine straight machine
stitches around the button embroideries
after they are cut out will help to prevent
the Aida fabric fraying while the buttons
are being made up. Take care to do the
machine stitching where it will not be seen
on the finished button.

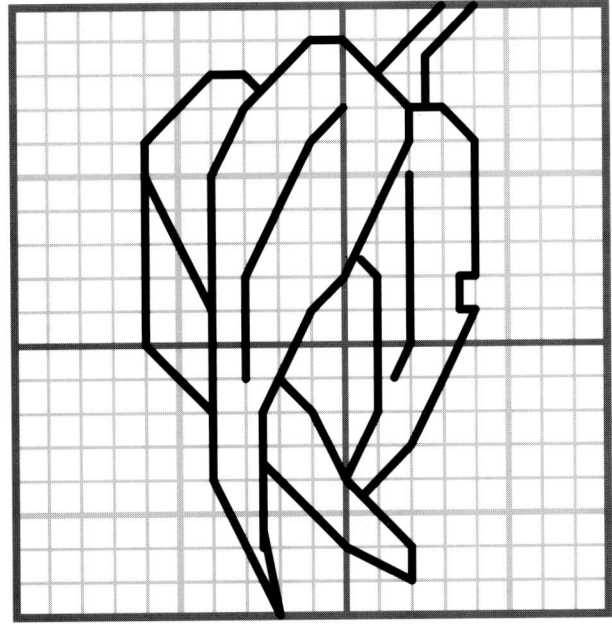

KEY
⌐ Fil Or gold

Flowers by Lisa Milasas

Canvas work cushion

Materials

DMC Pearl 3 Cotton (Art. 115) in the
    following quantities and colours:
    1 skein 320
    1 skein 349
    3 skeins 351
    1 skein 368
    1 skein 640
    2 skeins 642
    1 skein 644
DMC Tapestry Wool (Art. 486) in the
    following quantity and colour:
    27 skeins 7925
Zweigart Tapestry Canvas (Art. 604–48),
    48 × 48 cm
Tapestry needle, size 22
Chenille needle
Strong thread or wool
Embroidery scissors
Roller tapestry frame with taped beams
    50 cm long
Masking tape, 2.5 cm wide
Water spray
Wooden board (not particle board nor
    cork), at least 58 × 58 cm (see note)
Hammer
Nails, 20–25 mm
Cotton velveteen, sea green or blue
    colour, 50 cm
Medium-weight cotton fabric, coral
    colour, 30 cm
Machine thread to match velveteen and
    cotton fabrics
Piping cord, 2 metres
Cushion insert, 40 × 40 cm

To stop the embroidery threads becoming
snagged in the threads at the edge of the
canvas, cover the cut edges of the canvas
with masking tape.

Measure to find the centre of the cotton
tapes attached to the roller beams. Mark
the centre of each tape with a stitch or
indelible pen.

Find the centre of the two opposite edges
of the canvas that will be attached to the
roller beams. Mark the centre of each of
these two canvas edges.

Match the centre mark on one edge of the
canvas with the centre mark on one tape,
and stitch the canvas to the tape. Use a
running stitch — it doesn't have to be tiny,
1 cm stitches are fine — with a strong
thread or wool threaded onto a chenille
needle to make the job easier.

Before stitching the second end of the
canvas to the second beam, check that the
canvas is facing in the right direction.
Attach the other end of the canvas to the
tape on the other roller beam in the same
manner.

Wind the canvas around the beams so that the top of the canvas is visible between the beams. The canvas will be easier to stitch if it is drum tight on the frame. Lace the edges of the canvas to the side beams on the roller frame, and tighten the lacings so that the canvas is drum tight. These lacings may have to be tightened periodically to maintain the tension of the canvas.

When the embroidery on an area of canvas between the beams is complete, untie the lacings, wind the canvas on around a roller beam, and replace the lacings, before beginning the next section of embroidery. Measure 5 cm in and down from the top right-hand corner of the canvas. This point corresponds with the top right-hand corner of Chart 2. Start the background here (all the background is stitched in the tapestry wool). Use Continental Stitch for all the embroidery, following the stitch instructions on page 12. When the design is reached, count the pattern in following the chart (the design area is embroidered with pearl cotton).

When using the Pearl 3 cotton, take care to maintain the twist in the cotton, especially towards the end of each length of thread. Use lengths of thread which are approximately 50 cm long — an easy way is to untwist the skein and cut it at each end so that all the threads are ready-cut and of the correct length.

When the embroidery is complete, remove it from the roller frame.

Spray the back of the canvas with cold water. Don't saturate the canvas, but it should be wet.

Place the canvas right side down onto the blocking board. Nail two adjacent sides of the canvas to the board, keeping the edges of the canvas parallel with the edges of the board. Don't hammer the nails in far — four or five firm taps will do.

Nail the other two sides of the canvas to the board, pulling the canvas very tightly before hammering in the nails. The canvas should be nailed out square and as tight as possible onto the board.

Leave the canvas in an airy place out of the sun to dry thoroughly. (If you like, you can then leave the dry canvas on the board in a dry place until you are ready to make up the project.)

From the velveteen fabric, cut a square 45 × 45 cm for the back of the cushion. From the coral-coloured fabric, cut two metres of bias (as indicated in diagram, Piping 1).

Piping 1: Cut bias for piping

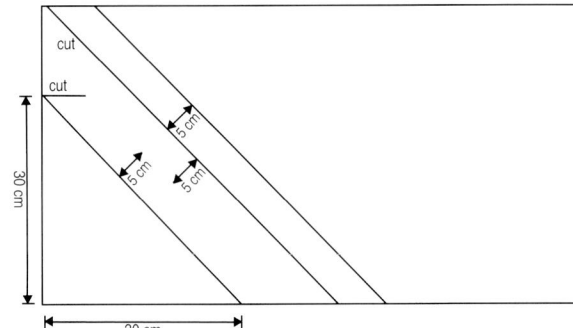

Join the bias strips, and machine stitch (see diagram, Piping 2).

Piping 2: Join bias strips

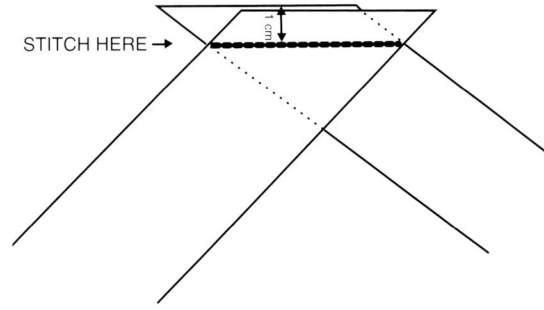

Press the seams open.

Fold the bias strip around the piping cord (as shown in diagram, Piping 3), and pin the cord into position. Place the zipper foot onto the sewing machine and straight stitch close to the cord.

The piping will be attached one row in from the edge of the needlepoint all around the cushion, so that the unstitched canvas will not show at the edge of the cushion. Begin by pinning the piping to the canvas work, starting halfway along the bottom edge of the design. The raw edge

Piping 3: Stitch piping

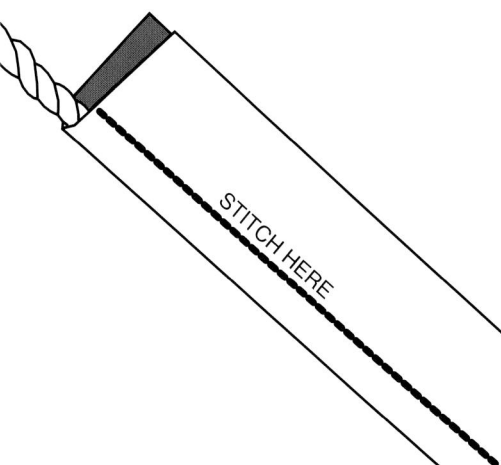

of the piping should face towards the outside edge of the canvas. Clip the seam allowances on the piping several times when attaching it to the corners, at the same time gently curve the piping around the corners. Pin the piping all around the cushion until the starting point is reached. Unpick a little stitching in the piping and join the two edges of the bias so they fit smoothly onto the cushion. Trim the seam allowances. Place the cord back into the bias, overlapping the ends of the cord in the channel (as shown in diagram, Piping 4).

Piping 4: Overlap the ends of the cord in the bias to join cord

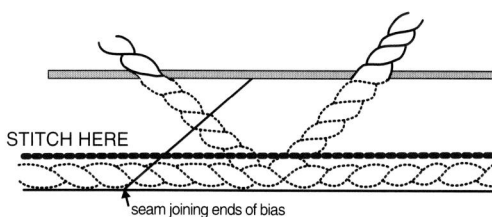

Machine stitch the join close to the cord, keeping the piping free of the canvas work. Pin the rest of the piping into place. Machine stitch the piping to the needlepoint, stitching close to the outer edge of the cord with the zipper foot on the sewing machine.
Press the backing fabric and place it on top of the piped canvas work, with right sides together. Pin the backing fabric into position close to the outer edge of the piping.

Machine stitch the backing to the canvas work on the outside of the piping cord, close to the piping cord, using the zipper foot on the sewing machine. On the bottom edge of the cushion, stitch only 3 cm around the bottom left and right corners, leaving a large gap unstitched. This gap is to turn the cushion and to insert the cushion filling.
Trim the seam allowances to 1 cm from the stitching.
Zigzag the raw edges of the cushion, taking care to zigzag each side of the gap in the lower edge of the cushion.
Turn the cushion right side out. Push the corners from the inside of the cushion. Place the insert into the cushion and slip stitch the opening closed.
Most specialist needlework shops offer a blocking and finishing service if you find the process too daunting!
NOTE: Particle board is not suitable as a blocking board as it is too hard; cork is too soft.

CHART 1

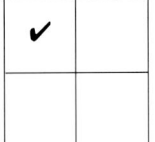

KEY

- ● 640 very dark beige grey
- ☒ 642 dark beige grey
- ◲ 644 medium beige grey
- ◪ 320 medium pistachio green
- ▣ 368 light pistachio green
- Ս 349 dark coral
- – 351 coral
- ☐ 7925 very dark peacock blue for background

CHART 2

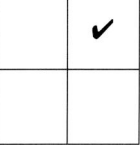

CHART 3

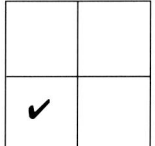

CHART 4

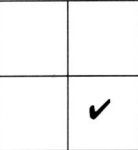

Classic doorstop

Materials

DMC Stranded Cotton (Art. 117) in the
 following quantities and colours:
  1 skein 320
  2 skeins 349
  3 skeins 351
  1 skein 368
  1 skein 640
  3 skeins 642
  1 skein 644
Aida (Art. 3706–589) Navy Blue, 52 × 40 cm
Tapestry needle, size 24
Embroidery scissors
Machine thread in a light colour
Medium-weight cotton fabric, navy blue
  colour, 30 x 20 cm
Machine cotton to match
Brick or heavy piece of wood to fit the
  embroidery (see note)
Polyester wadding
Strong thread or wool for lacing
Straw needle, size 3 or 4

Zigzag by machine or oversew by hand
around the cut edges of the Aida fabric.
Fold the fabric in half both ways and tack
centre lines across the fabric in each direction.
You may prefer to photocopy the charts
and tape them together before starting the
embroidery.
Find the centre of the taped charts, and
start the Cross Stitch embroidery here (follow
the Cross Stitch instructions on page 9).
When the embroidery is complete, remove
the tacked centre lines and press the fabric
on the wrong side.
Cut two pieces of polyester wadding to fit
each of the six sides of the brick or wooden
block. Oversew the pieces of wadding
together by hand and place the doorstop
form inside before stitching the last sides
closed.
Pin the side seams of the doorstop together
and slip it over the doorstop to check that
it fits snugly. Adjust if necessary. Machine
stitch the side seams. Trim the side seam
allowances on the Aida fabric. Turn the
embroidery right side out, and slip it over
the padded doorstop. Lace the opposite
sides of the Aida fabric together across the
bottom of the doorstop with the strong
thread or wool.
Press the navy blue cotton fabric and place
it on the bottom of the doorstop with right
side out. Turn under the raw edges, so that
the fabric fits the bottom of the doorstop,
and slip stitch the fabric into position,
using a doubled length of navy blue
machine thread in the straw needle.
NOTE: If using a brick it will have to be
completely dry. It may need baking in the
oven to dry it out thoroughly.

CHART 1

KEY
- ● 640 very dark beige grey
- ☒ 642 dark beige grey
- ◹ 644 medium beige grey
- ☑ 320 medium pistachio green
- ☐ 368 light pistachio green
- Ⓤ 349 very dark salmon
- ⊟ 351 dark salmon

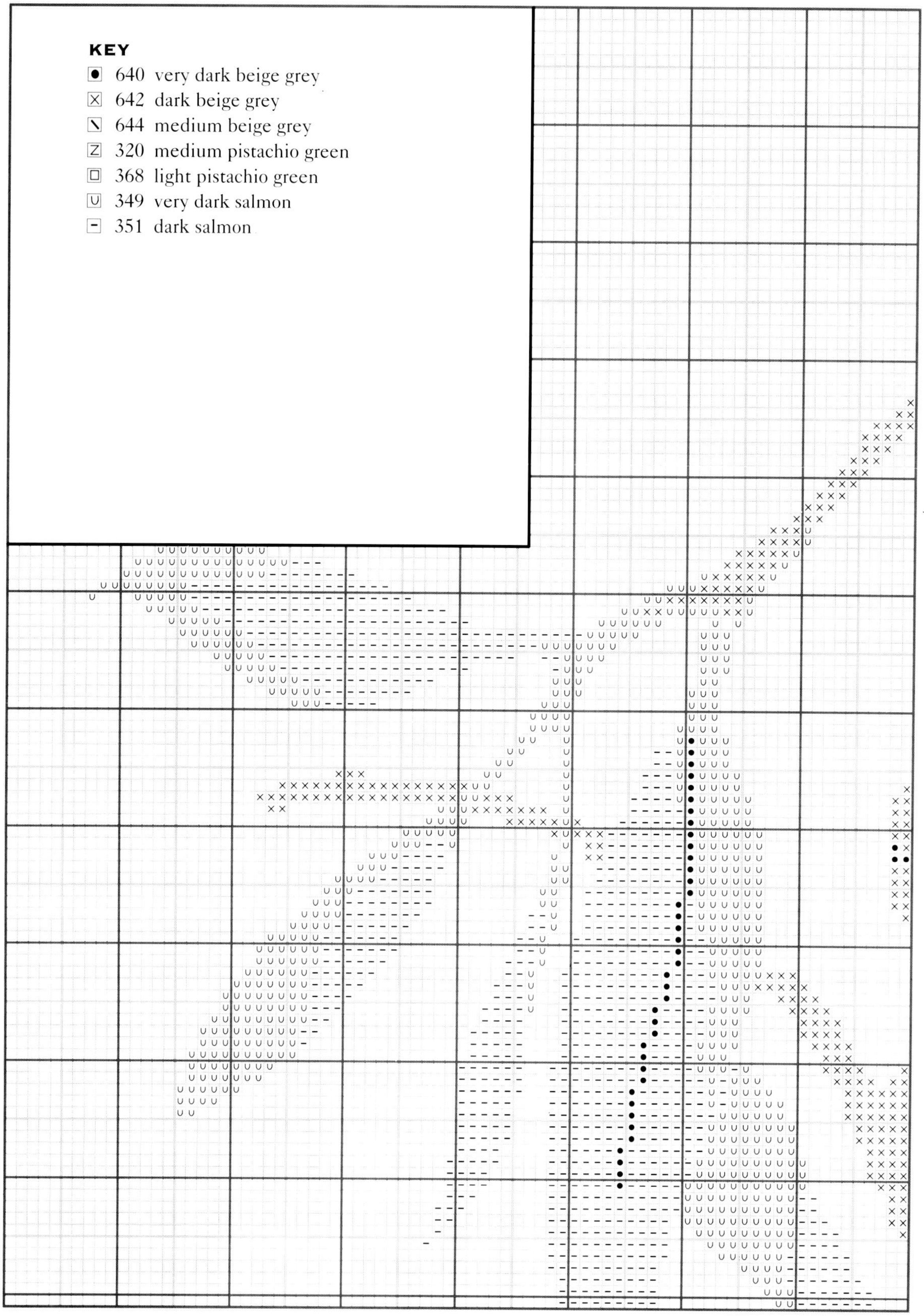

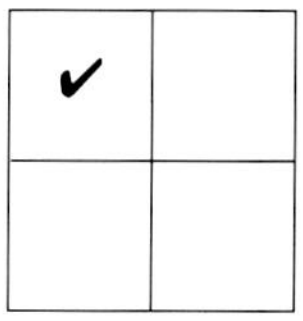

CHART 2

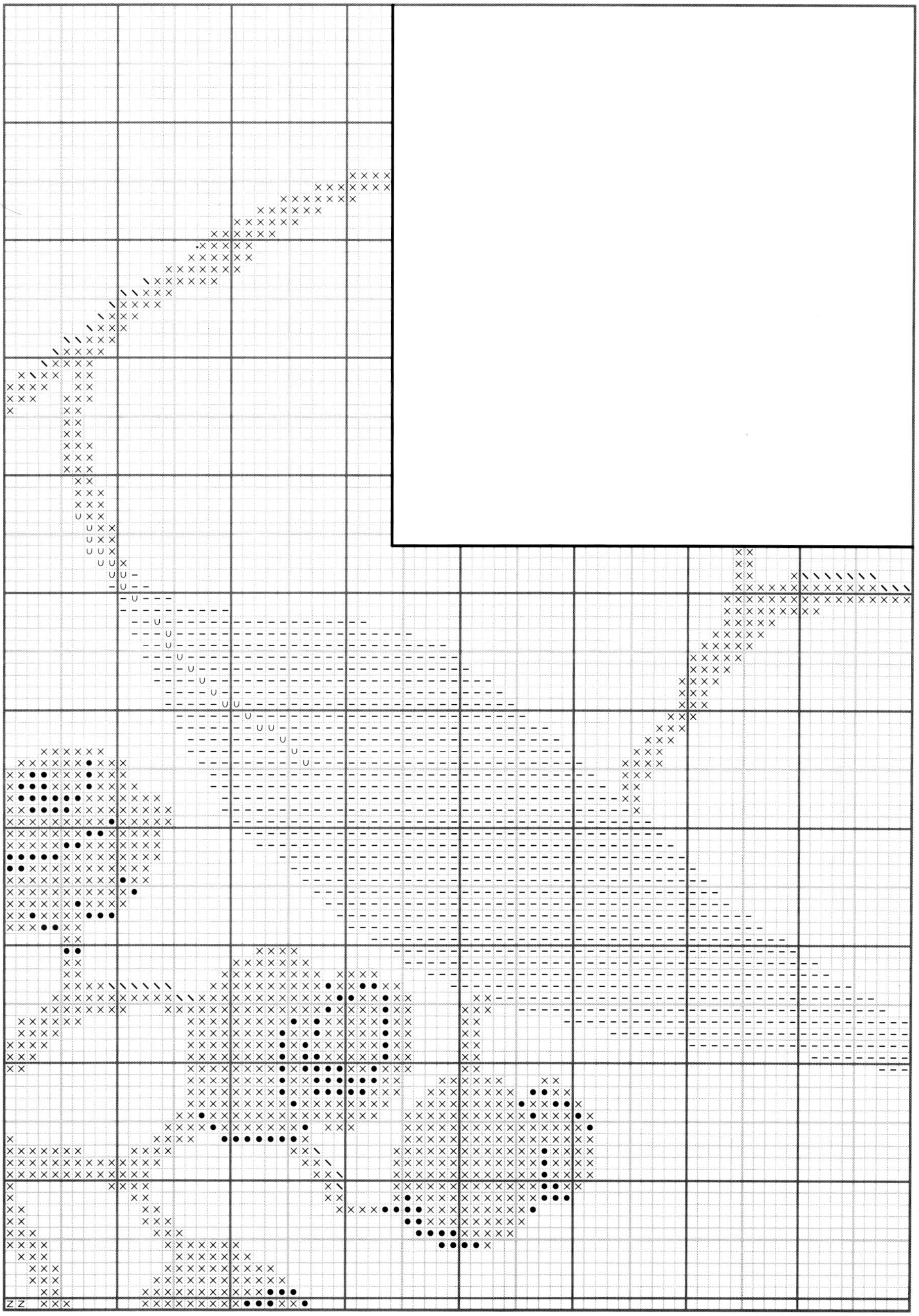

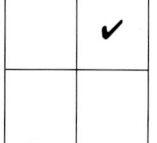

CHART 3

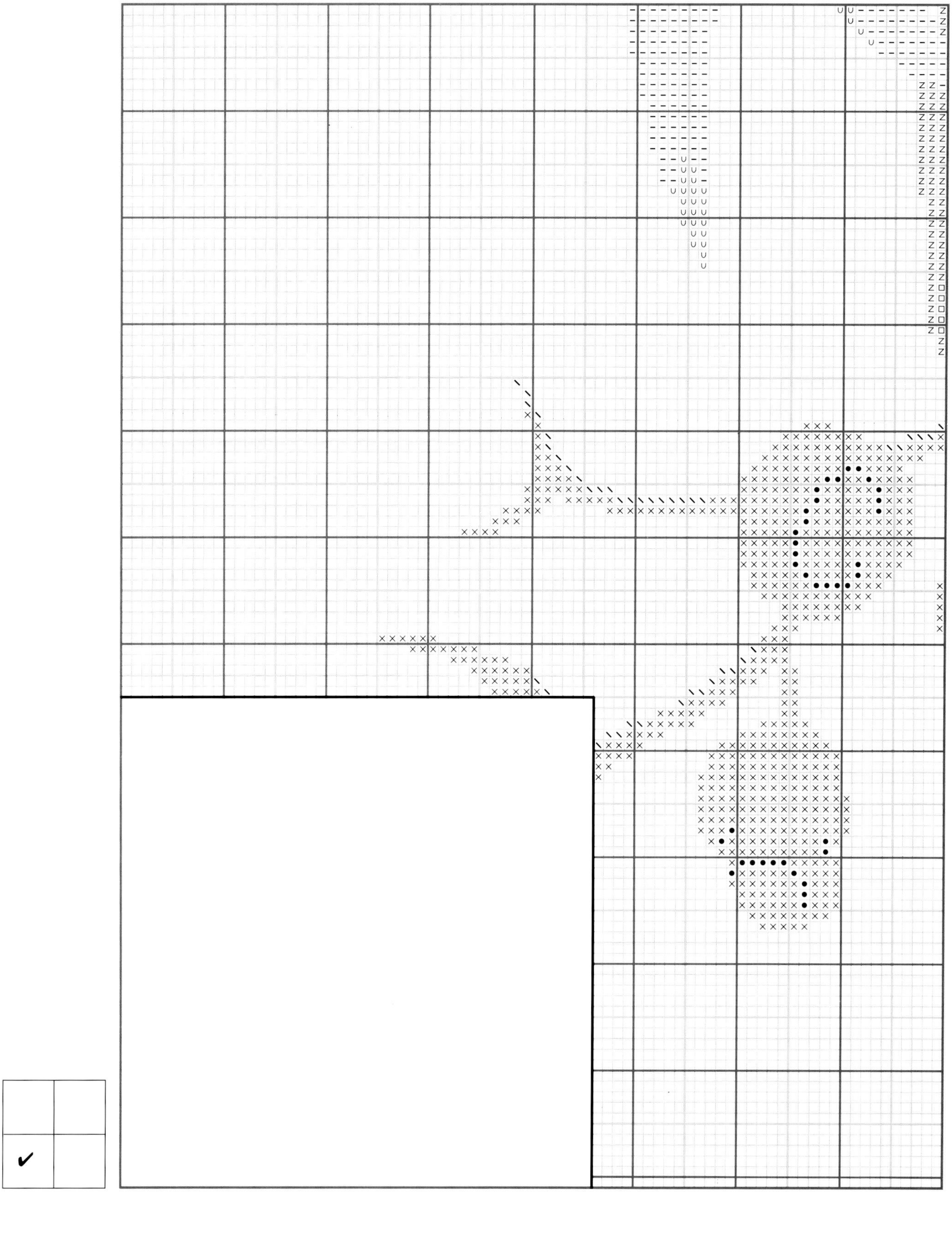

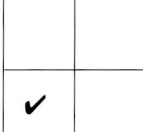

CHART 4

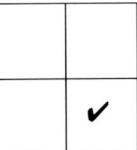

Flowers by Lisa Milasas

Wildflower picture

Materials

DMC Flower Threads (Art. 106) in the following quantities and colours:

1 skein 2320
1 skein 2354
1 skein 2356
1 skein 2369
1 skein 2472
1 skein 2610
1 skein 2727r
1 skein 2734
1 skein 2745
1 skein 2759
1 skein 2766
1 skein 2783
1 skein 2815
1 skein 2907
1 skein 2918
1 skein 2986
2 skeins 2890

Dublin Linen (Art. 3604–101) Antique White, 34 × 44 cm
Machine thread in a medium colour
Tapestry needle, size 24
Embroidery scissors

Zigzag by machine or oversew by hand around the cut edges of the linen.

Find the centre of the linen and tack centre lines each way across the linen using the machine thread.

Find the centre of the chart and start the embroidery here. The centre of the linen corresponds with the centre of the charted design.

Follow the Cross Stitch instructions on page 9.

When the embroidery is complete, remove the tacking lines. Press the embroidery on the wrong side, and have it framed.

CHART 1

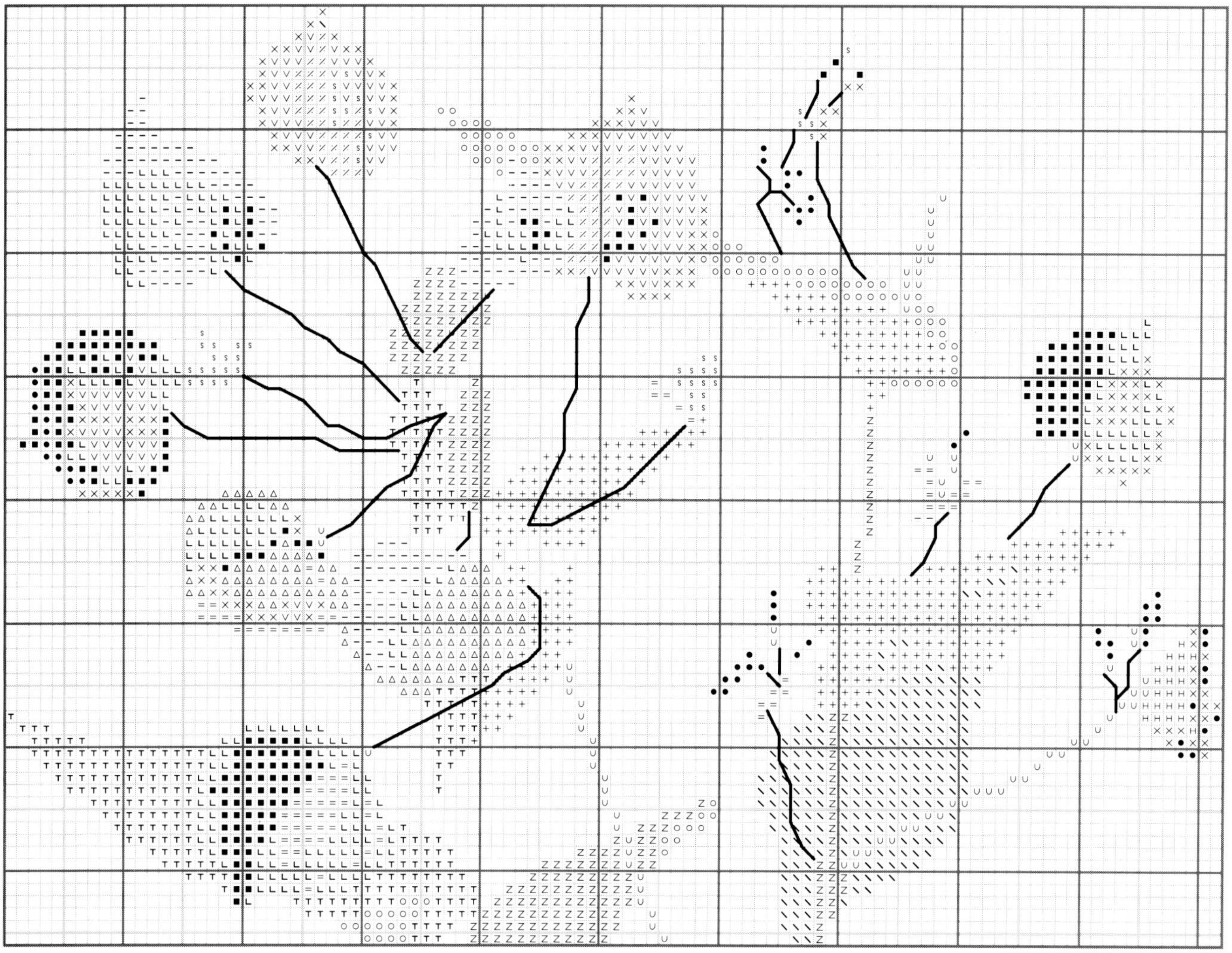

KEY

⊞	2986	very dark forest green
◣	2472	ultra light avocado green
◪	2890	ultra dark pistachio green
T	2320	medium pistachio green
◯	2369	very light pistachio green
U	2734	light olive green
S	2907	light parrot green
◿	2610	very dark drab brown
–	2759	ultra very light terracotta

L	2356	medium terracotta
■	2354	dark brick pink
●	2815	medium garnet
H	2918	dark red copper
V	2766	medium sandstone orange
⊠	2783	medium topaz
⊟	2727	very light topaz
△	2745	light pale yellow

CHART 2

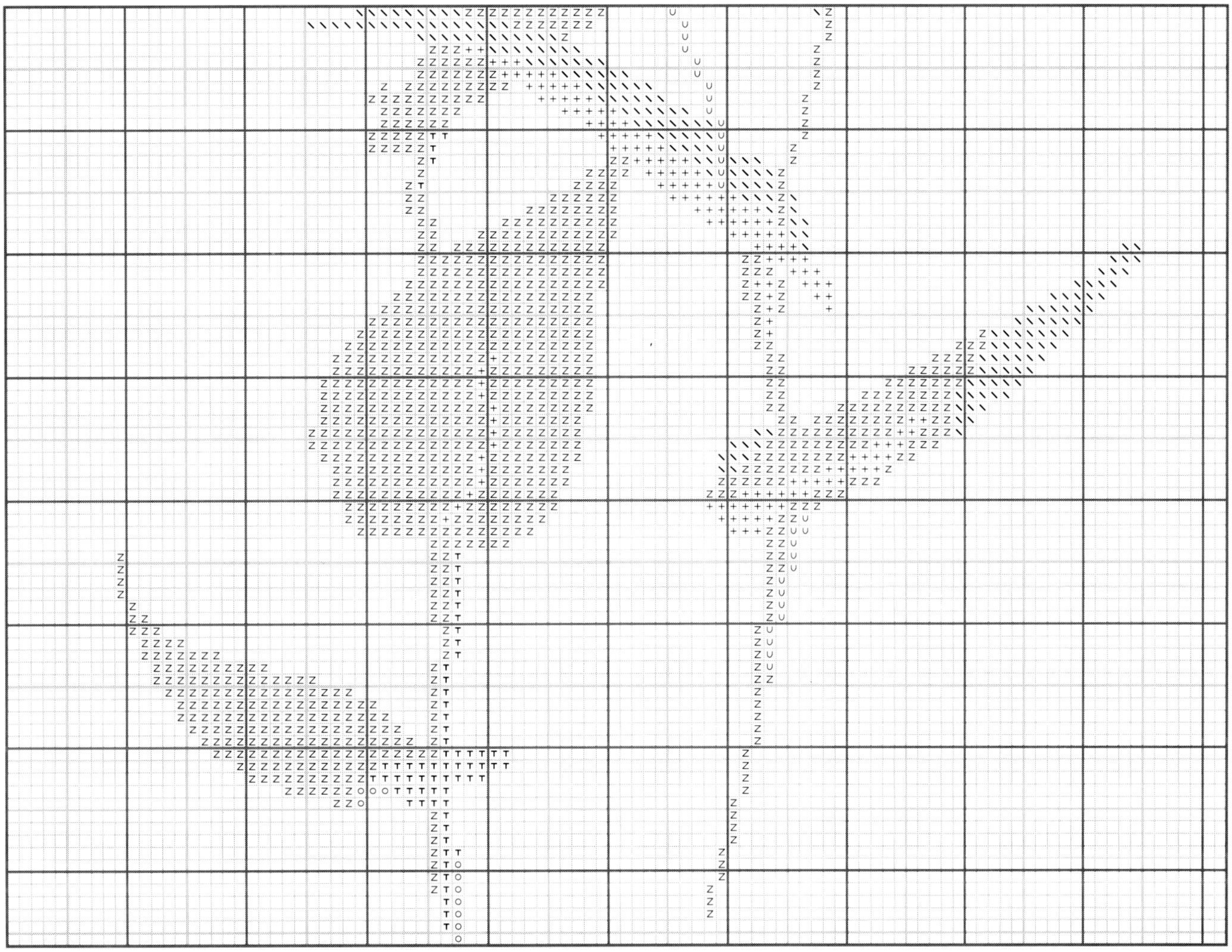

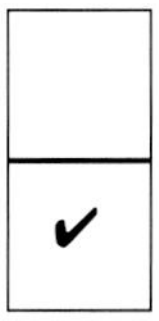

*May Gibbs — naturalist, psychologist and artist explorer has mapped
out a world of her own and conquered it completely.*

ADELAIDE ADVERTISER 1918

Tales of Snugglepot and Cuddlepie was combined with its two sequels, *Little Ragged Blossom* and *Little Obelia*, in 1940. Since then the *Complete Adventures of Snugglepot and Cuddlepie* has never been out of print and the magic of the May Gibbs characters still enchants children and adults today. Harper Collins Publishers produce a range of beautiful children's books, stationery items and craft titles featuring the ever popular May Gibbs characters.

Complete Adventures of Snugglepot and Cuddlepie

The Story of Little Obelia

The Story of Little Ragged Blossom

Snugglepot and Cuddlepie

Tiny Story of Snugglepot and Cuddlepie

Tiny Story of Little Obelia

Tiny Bush Babies

May Gibbs Address Book

May Gibbs Alphabet Book

Alphabet Frieze

May Gibbs Baby Book

May Gibbs Birthday Book

May Gibbs Counting Book

MAY GIBBS AND VICKY KITANOV

Ten Little Gumnuts

Ten Little Gumnuts Frieze

Ten Little Gumnuts Miniature

A Gumnuts Year

Other titles in the Bay Books series

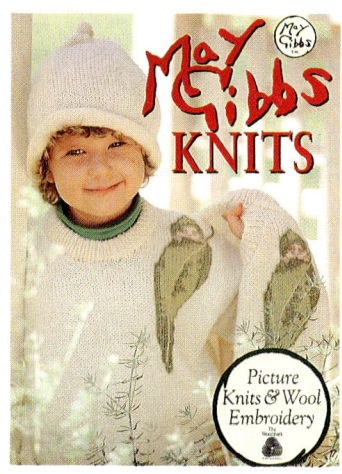

May Gibbs Knits

Fabulous picture knits and wool embroidery, for children and adults, created around May Gibbs' enchanting illustrations.
Create jumpers featuring Australia's favourite bushland characters: Sweet Pea, Little Ragged Blossom, Mrs Bear and the Wattle Baby, Snugglepot and Cuddlepie.
Knit a delightful Gum Nut Baby jumper, cardigan, and hat.
Knit and embroider exquisite jumpers and cardigans detailing gum nuts, gum leaves, boronia, wattle and gum blossoms, and delphiniums.
ISBN 1 86378 005 X

May Gibbs Country Craft

A selection of beautiful projects for you to make, created around May Gibbs' characters and bushland images. Includes full-size designs and a pull-out pattern sheet.
Paint in the folk-art style to decorate a bread board and key holder, dining-chair backs, serviette rings, a wall plaque, coathangers, a plant pot, watering can, hat band, and garden apron.
Decoupage candlesticks, coathangers, a platter, bookmark, and tea tray.
Stencil place mats, coathangers, a wall frieze, height chart, and cushion.
ISBN 1 86378 052 1

May Gibbs Needlepoint

Bring her delightful characters and flowers into your home, with this wonderful range of needlepoint projects to suit all tastes and skill levels.
Make a Gumnut Town library bag, a Wattle Baby or Little Ragged Blossom doll, Flannel Flowers or Sweet Pea glasses case, Gumleaves workbag, Delphinium tiebacks for curtains, a Little Ragged Blossom box, Baby Faces or Gumleaves doorstop, a rambling flowers picture, and six elegant cushions.
ISBN 1 86378 0 53 X

The publisher has made every effort to ensure that all details were correct at the time of printing.

PROJECT MANAGER
Kate Tully

STYLIST
Louise Owens

PHOTOGRAPHER
Andrew Elton

STITCHERS
Betty Buckley, Jenny Burman, Pat Lance, Georgina McCarthy, Joan Smith, Alison Snepp, Kerry Stibbe

CHARTS
David Marsh and John Snepp

ACKNOWLEDGMENTS
All DMC threads, Zweigart canvas, evenweave linen and Aida fabrics from:
DMC Needlecraft Pty Ltd
PO Box 317
Earlwood NSW 2206
tel (02) 559 3088

Framecraft bowl from:
Ireland Needlecraft
PO Box 1175
Narre Warren VIC 3803
tel (03) 702 3222

Wildflower Picture framing by Laszlo for:
Janet's Art Supplies
145 Victoria Avenue
Chatswood NSW 2067
tel (02) 417 5405

All flowers from:
Lisa Milasas
300 Sylvania Road
Gymea NSW 2227
tel 018 166 087

Tray on page 28 from:
Victoria's Old Charm Antiques
82 Sydney Street
Willoughby NSW 2068
tel (02) 419 7008

A Bay Books Publication

Bay Books, an imprint of HarperCollins*Publishers*
25 Ryde Road, Pymble NSW 2073, Australia
31 View Road, Glenfield, Auckland 10, New Zealand

First published in Australia in 1994
May Gibbs work and patterns copyright © Spastic Centre of NSW and NSW Society for Children and Young Adults with Physical Disabilities 1994

National Library of Australia
Cataloguing-in-Publication data:

Snepp, Alison
  May Gibbs Embroidery.
  ISBN 1 86378 054 8.
  1.Embroidery–Patterns. I.Gibbs, May, 1877–1969.
  II.Title
746.44041

Printed in Australia by Griffin Press, Netley, SA
9 8 7 6 5 4 3 2 1
97 96 95 94